PHOTO BY BERT ANDREWS

James Noble, Stephen Joyce, Sloane Shelton, Craig Richard Nelson and Joseph Mathewson in a scene from the New York production of "The Runner Stumbles." Setting by Patricia Woodbridge.

# THE RUNNER STUMBLES

### A PLAY IN TWO ACTS
### BY MILAN STITT

**DRAMATISTS
PLAY SERVICE
INC.**

## SOUND EFFECTS RECORDS

The following sound effects records, which may be used in
connection with production of this play, can be obtained from
Thomas J. Valentino, Inc., 151 West 46th Street, New York,
N. Y. 10036.

> No. 4027—Dog barking
> No. 5004—Fire alarm
> No. 5005—Church bell
> No. 5006—Wind
> No. 5020—Train whistle
> No. 5198—Clock ticking

For T.A.L.

## ABOUT THE AUTHOR

Milan Stitt based *The Runner Stumbles* on an actual turn of the century trial for the murder of a nun in Michigan. He first developed the play in the Boston University Playwrights Workshop at the Berkshire Theatre Festival, and then in a showcase production at the Manhattan Theatre Club in 1974. It received its world premiere at the Hartman Theatre Company in Stamford, Connecticut, on December 30, 1975, and opened on Broadway at the Little Theatre on May 18, 1976. Mr. Stitt is a founder and executive director of Triad Playwrights Company, an Off Off Broadway group which helps writers develop new plays. In addition to teaching Triad's playwriting class, he has produced for Triad plays by Ross Alexander, Robert Esposito, Richard Greene and D.B. Gilles' *The Girl Who Loved the Beatles*. Mr. Stitt's one-character play, *Edie's Home*, was presented by Triad, and subsequently taped and broadcast by WBAI. Off-Broadway he coproduced *Kiss Now*, a rock musical. He has held administrative positions with the American Shakespeare Festival, Long Wharf Theatre and American Place Theatre. He studied with Kenneth Rowe at the University of Michigan, where he won two Avery Hopwood Playwriting Awards, and with John Gassner at the Yale School of Drama. He was born in Detroit, Michigan, and now lives in the Chelsea section of New York City.

THE RUNNER STUMBLES opened on Broadway at the Little Theatre on May 18, 1976. It was directed by Austin Pendleton, and the set was by Patricia Woodbridge, costumes by James Berton Harris and lighting by Cheryl Thacker. The producers were Wayne Adams and Willard Morgan by special arrangement with The Hartman Theatre Company; production stage manager, Peggy Peterson; general manager, Dorothy Olim; and author's assistant, Martin Lee Koslow. The cast in order of appearance was:

| | |
|---|---|
| AMOS | Morrie Piersol |
| FATHER RIVARD | Stephen Joyce |
| ERNA PRINDLE | Katina Commings |
| TOBY FELKER | James Noble |
| SISTER RITA | Nancy Donohue |
| MRS. SHANDIG | Sloane Shelton |
| PROSECUTOR | Craig Richard Nelson |
| MONSIGNOR NICHOLSON | Joseph Mathewson |
| LOUISE | Marilyn Pfeiffer |

THE RUNNER STUMBLES was first developed in workshop in the Boston University Playwrights Project at the Berkshire Theatre Festival in July 1971 under the direction of Pirie MacDonald; Mouzon Law, Executive Director. It was further developed in a showcase production at the Manhattan Theatre Club in December 1976 under the direction of Austin Pendleton; Lynn Meadow, Executive Director. It received its world premiere at the Hartman Theatre Company on December 30, 1975 under the direction of Austin Pendleton; Del and Margot Tenney, Executive Directors.

THE RUNNER STUMBLES was suggested by an actual turn of the century trial for the murder of a nun in Michigan.

TIME: April 1911.

PLACE: A cell, courthouse and grave in Solon, Michigan.

For reading ease, Father Rivard is called *Rivard* in the present tense scenes, and *Priest* in past-tense scenes. There are a few bracketed sections in the second act which were cut from the Broadway production, but may be appropriately utilized for subsequent productions.

# The Runner Stumbles

## ACT I

AT RISE: *The mournful wail of a distant train whistle is heard, followed by the Prosecutor's Voice at the arraignment: "Then may this matter of the People of the State of Michigan versus Brian Rivard be set down for immediate trial."*

*Guard leads Rivard from* U. C. *to cell* D. R. *Half way to the cell Rivard stops and looks around as furniture is briefly lighted. Guard urges him forward finally pushing Rivard in cell.*

*Rivard is in a state that exaggerated would be catatonic. He just wants to be left alone. He wears handcuffs.*

## THE CELL

*(Rivard looks up at cell window as he hears children singing "The Lilac Song.")* *

GUARD. That's the children singing at the school, Father.

RIVARD. (*Sits on* L. *stool.*) You hear it too? (*Erna enters* U. L.)

GUARD. Ain't deaf, Father.

RIVARD. No. That's not what I— See, for a moment I thought. . . . Sister Rita taught that song, but I couldn't possibly hear voices from up on the hill, could I?

GUARD. No. It's from the public school down here. (*Sound of children singing fades.*) There ain't been no Catholic school up there since you ran off. (*Guard is about to sit on* R. *stool when he sees Erna. She carries a napkin which holds muffins.*) Erna. What are you doing back here?

RIVARD. Erna.

GUARD. (*Crosses* U. *of Rivard.*) You ain't ever supposed to come back here.

* *See note at back of playbook.*

7

ERNA. (*Enters cell* R.) I have to, Amos. I have to. You don't understand, Amos. Please. Leave me alone a minute. (*Guard remains.*) I'll be all right. I will. (*Guard exits* U. L. *Erna tentatively approaches cell.*)

RIVARD. Hello, Erna. Thank you for coming.

ERNA. (*Sits on* R. *stool, crosses herself in preparation for confession.*) Father. Let me tell the truth right out. I haven't been to Confession for four and a half years.

RIVARD. Erna. I can't.

ERNA. Of course, you can, Father.

RIVARD. What's that, Erna? What do you have there?

ERNA. (*Handing him napkin with muffins.*) For you. I made it up special. Your favorite.

RIVARD. Mince meat muffins.

ERNA. Yes, yes. I knew you'd remember. I cook for the prisoners here. We live just up the road. The yellow house. Right in town now 'cause I'm married, Father. Maurice Prindle. He's thirty years older, but we have three children already. So it takes a lot, and I cook for them here.

RIVARD. That's good.

ERNA. Maurice isn't Catholic.

RIVARD. I remember.

ERNA. But it's wrong.

RIVARD. Marriage, if you're happy, if it does that, Erna, how can it be wrong? (*Guard enters* U. L.)

ERNA. If you look out your window, Father, you can see Holy Rosary Church up on the hill. I can see it from my kitchen. If you're troubled or scared, you can just stand and look at it. It's a comfort, a real comfort.

GUARD. (U. *of Rivard and Erna.*) You better get moving, Erna. His lawyer just came and is talking with the sheriff. Then he'll be coming back here. (*Lawyer enters* U. L.)

ERNA. (*Kneeling* R. *of Rivard.*) Everyone says you did it, Father, but they don't know you the way I did.

GUARD. Come on, Erna.

RIVARD. Do you think I'm guilty, Erna? That I could kill Sister Rita?

ERNA. (*Uncertain.*) No.

GUARD. Erna. He's here. (*Erna exits.*)

LAWYER. (*Enters cell, attempts to shake hands with handcuffed*

8

*Rivard.*) Toby Felker. Oh, come on, Amos. (*Guard removes hand-cuffs.*) Don't pay him any mind. Young men hereabouts don't amount to much, and I don't know why. I was burning up with ambition when I was their age. (*To Guard.*) You can wait outside now.

GUARD. Have to protect you, Toby.

LAWYER. You have to listen so you can tell that crowd out there what's happening. You go out right now or I'm telling the sheriff—

GUARD. (*Eating a muffin.*) If you take him for your lawyer, you better be sure you're pleading guilty 'cause he ain't ever got nobody off, everybody knows it, too.

LAWYER. (*Calling.*) Sheriff.

GUARD. Toby. I was going to do a chore anyway. (*Guard exits U. L. taking muffins.*)

LAWYER. The circuit judge appointed me to take your case. You don't remember me, do you? I met you once. A Grange meeting in Leland. You were sharp as a pin at the Grange. Explaining why Catholics have Mass and everything. Don't you remember? I was the one who introduced you and conducted the question and answer period. (*Sits on R. stool.*) Now I got to tell you, you don't have to make me as your lawyer. You don't. But if you don't, you should know, for one thing, I'm the only lawyer out here on the peninsula. Now there isn't much for a lawyer out here, you know. 'Cept after the spring rains move the creeks hither and thither. Arguing boundary disputes, if you know what I mean. But you don't have to take me. Maurice told me the smelt are running down at Boyne City, and I wouldn't mind getting a barrel of 'em. You fish?

RIVARD. Do you want my case?

LAWYER. Sure. Sure I want your case. (*Standing.*) Do you accept me? That's the point.

RIVARD. (*Standing.*) As long as you believe I'm innocent.

LAWYER. Innocent?

RIVARD. Yes.

LAWYER. But that means a trial. And I'd have to know, well, a lot. Yes. A lot. (*He sits. Takes old envelope from pocket on which to make notes.*) What did happen that last day? The day of the fire. Four and a half years ago. You both disappeared the same night. Everyone figured . . . but you tell me, what did happen?

9

RIVARD. (*Crosses u. of stool.*) I don't know. I know nothing happened. It couldn't have. I'm not a violent man. (*Rivard sits.*)

LAWYER. All right. All right. We could start at the beginning. Why did you send for another nun? (*Nun appears at bottom of ramp.*)

RIVARD. The other two sisters were ill.

LAWYER. Did you ask for a young one?

RIVARD. There was so much she'd have to . . . (*Turning, half speaking to Nun.*) I can't live through it again.

LAWYER. Exactly when did she arrive?

RIVARD. About this time of year. There were lilacs. It seemed late. I mean, I had expected her about an hour earlier. (*Nun carrying rattan suitcase and some lilacs starts up ramp.*) I walked out to the road to see if I could see her coming up from the valley. No. (*Nun stops.*) That's all.

NUN. I didn't think it would be beautiful. All those trees. (*Sound of dog barking down in the toylike town.*) It's almost a wilderness.

LAWYER. How can I help you if . . .

RIVARD. Some other time. We'll talk some other. . . .

NUN. (*Overlapping Rivard, as she steps onto stage.*) I barely slept on the train for imagining what Solon would be like.

RIVARD. No. No. I don't want to remember.

NUN. Every house down there has lilacs, doesn't it? I picked these down there along the road. The Bishop told me the Indian name for Solon was Land of Rainbows.

## THE HILL

(*Rivard crosses to Nun with an abrupt change of attitude. He is open, vigorous, truly pleased to see Nun.*)

PRIEST. (*Accepting lilacs from Nun.*) Yes, they're fond of Indian names at the Chancery, but it has been a long time since there's been a rainbow in Solon. We're experiencing a drought. But they wouldn't know that.

NUN. That's why there are no birds. It's so peculiar, all those trees and not a single bird. You can almost smell the dryness.

PRIEST. According to Indian superstition the birds leave before a forest fire.

NUN. Oh, I hope not, Father. In Detroit, where I grew up, there were just scraggly trees along the street. Now this forest. . . .

10

PRIEST. You'll weary of the trees, Sister. The winter is long up here, and the trees sometimes seem to be closing in on you. I find the best thing to do is to just keep busy. Then there's no time for homesickness or any melancholy over what you renounced. You won't want that in your mind up here. Not because of any rule, but just because it might slow you down.

NUN. They used to say that at Guardian Angel as if it would comfort me. But I don't believe it, Father. It was a new life when I entered the convent, yes. But I was alive before. I believe everything I've done is part of me. I had to be a child then to be a nun now. I've kept a diary. Since I was old enough to write really. When I look through it now, I see that most of the worries I had at fifteen, I have today. I am a person who is a nun, not a nun who used to be a person.

PRIEST. (*Picking up suitcase.*) Well, Mrs. Shandig is my housekeeper. Neither Sister Immaculata nor Sister Mary Martha have been well lately so Mrs. Shandig can help you to—

NUN. I shouldn't have spoken so plainly. I've angered you.

PRIEST. Not at all.

NUN. Would you wait then?

PRIEST. Why?

NUN. You're annoyed with me.

PRIEST. I'm not annoyed.

NUN. But you seem so—

PRIEST. What do you want?

NUN. The Church. There is a certain prayer—I promised my saint it would be the first—

PRIEST. You certainly don't need to apologize for praying.

NUN. Father. Please don't be angry before you know me.

PRIEST. I am not angry. Except by the fact that you keep telling me that I am.

NUN. I'm sorry. (*Silence.*)

PRIEST. The other sisters, they never talk much. At least not with me, but then what could they . . . But I do enjoy exchanging ideas. I do. But the people up here. They respect the Church, but they expect that priests . . . You know. I think I'm out of practice.

NUN. I think conversation is as essential as air. If people don't talk with each other, what good is anything?

11

PRIEST. You know when I first came to Solon I too made a completely terrible start.

NUN. I don't feel I've made a completely terrible start.

PRIEST. No. No, you haven't. I didn't mean that. But when I came to Solon, I was the first priest appointed to Holy Rosary in nine years. The Bishop didn't even know if the Church would still be here. But you know how eager Bishop Ginter is to expand, which is why I think he sent me here. And also I needed a quiet parish to work on my book. It's called "Augustinian Order (colon) An Examination and Extension." And surprisingly enough, what with starting the school, convincing the men to build the convent, converting one of them in the process, and . . . well, the book is coming along. Not as fast as I'd hoped because . . . At any rate, when I arrived here, no one met me. I asked the blacksmith for directions. Maurice Prindle, the blacksmith, is rather a practical joker and he sent me to that little church down here. And when I saw the sign "Solon Evangelical Methodist" (*As they laugh, he hands her suitcase. Nun exits* U. L.)

## THE CELL

LAWYER. (*Standing.*) Rivard, listen to me.

RIVARD. (*Crossing to Lawyer.*) I did not kill Sister Rita. There's very little to hold on to. I've doubted my sanity at moments. I believe in God, the Father Almighty. There's that. But I don't have the Church, all the helps that other— She haunted me.

LAWYER. Rivard. Let's just say. Let's just say, I don't understand, Rivard.

RIVARD. She did. When I left here. For a long time it kept—

LAWYER. (*Putting Rivard on* R. *stool.*) Rivard. Get ahold of yourself. (*Lawyer sits on* L. *stool.*)

RIVARD. It's true. She never left my side. No matter what I did. I needed some kind of order. In Detroit I worked on the assembly line. I worked very hard. There's endless overtime, you see, and I took it all just so I wouldn't think. I moved my hands back and forth and the shiny parts came and went on the two black belts. Just so I'd be tired, and could sleep. But it failed. The harder I worked, the more I saw her.

LAWYER. Sister Rita.

RIVARD. Yes. I'd go to the room at night and I would fall asleep,

12

but then my hands would just start moving, working like in the factory, back and forth. From the assembly line, you know. And then I'd be awake. The room was black, empty, but there would be this lightness, a presence, her. I thought maybe it was the place. Maybe by some coincidence she had lived near that place when she was a girl. It had those scraggly trees which she had talked about. So I moved. I moved so many times. And then, now, the last few months it's . . . abated. And I'm afraid to have it back. I can't.

LAWYER. Father, do you hear yourself? You talk like a guilty man.

RIVARD. You don't understand. You see the only time I actually approached happiness was during these last few months in Detroit. No one knew my name. No one expected anything of me. I want to live like that again. Working. Walking. Eating. Sleeping. No past. No future. Just a very small present.

LAWYER. That's the kind of thinking your theology gets you into, Father. See I understand something about you Catholics. And I don't mind. I believe you are innocent. I don't know why. Just instinct, I guess. What you people call a leap of faith. But I've got to have hard facts, Father. Now I don't suppose there's any way I could get the jury to believe the nun commited suicide.

RIVARD. No.

LAWYER. Now she was dead when you left, right?

RIVARD. (*Standing.*) They told me in Detroit when they arrested me. I didn't know she died.

LAWYER. She was alive when you left.

RIVARD. Yes.

LAWYER. (*Standing.*) You're certain.

RIVARD. Yes.

LAWYER. Then that's it.

RIVARD. What?

LAWYER. Your defense. I got it. I have got it. It doesn't matter *why*, but *when* you left. And *who* saw you who can testify she was still alive. The other nuns? How in the hell do you suppose you subpoena nuns? Remember that day, Father. Who? Who saw you leave that knows you left before Sister Rita was killed? You had to come through town, right? Who saw you? Maurice? He's always sitting out front.

13

RIVARD. Yes. I talked to him. Maurice. I asked, I asked him to do a chore for me up at Holy Rosary.

LAWYER. Good. (*Calling.*) Amos.

RIVARD. Yes. I can remember. You'll help me. I am strong enough. I'll remember every detail, and then it will be over.

LAWYER. (*Shaking Rivard's hand.*) Now that I've got a handle on this, I know I can do good work. I'm good. (*Guard enters* u. l.) Hell, I'm already better than I thought I'D be. (*Excited, Lawyer begins to exit* u. l. *with Guard, then turns back.*) Good bye, for now. (*Guard and Lawyer exit. Rivard hears children singing "The Lilac Song." Rivard turns* u. *to listen, and watches Mrs. Shandig enter* u. l. *The singing turns into the sound of children laughing as Rivard crosses to desk where he sits. Mrs. Shandig leaves her kitchen to see what the laughing is all about. When she is* d. l. *of* c., *Nun enters* d. r. *and crosses, nearly running with school papers. Mrs. Shandig startles Nun when she speaks.*)

## BACK PORCH

MRS. SHANDIG. Sister. What's wrong?

NUN. Mrs. Shandig, don't tell father. I forgot their compositions so I ran back to the convent while—

MRS. SHANDIG. But the noise, Sister. And laughing.

NUN. Yes. It's Louise doing her celebrated imitation of me. You could have watched them for me. I never even thought o— (*Sound begins to fade.*)

MRS. SHANDIG. Oh, no. I never go to the school.

NUN. (*Showing her composition.*) This is Louise's. Look at that. She writes so well.

MRS. SHANDIG. Oh yes. It's very neat.

NUN. Just read a little of it. I have to get back. You'll see how well she—

MRS. SHANDIG. (*Starting to exit.*) No. I don't have time.

NUN. (*Stopping her.*) Mrs. Shandig?

MRS. SHANDIG. Yes.

NUN. Oh just . . . remember, if you ever want to sit in the back of class to listen, to the singing or whatever—

MRS. SHANDIG. Sister, Sister, ever since you came, I wanted to ask you . . .

NUN. What?

MRS. SHANDIG. Father doesn't have to teach since you're here, but he works even harder on his book since you came. I worry about him.

NUN. Why?

MRS. SHANDIG. He's in that study from Mass til supper most days. And I thought if I could read some of the books for him, I could tell him what's in them and then he wouldn't get so tired and irritable. I want to help him, but I don't . . . Well, you see . . .

NUN. I could teach you to read, Mrs. Shandig.

MRS. SHANDIG. Do you think I can learn reading?

NUN. Of course.

MRS. SHANDIG. I am older you know.

NUN. Anyone who knows the entire Mass by heart . . . I saw your lips following the Mass.

MRS. SHANDIG. I wasn't always . . . I'm only a convert, Sister. Father Rivard, he brought me into the Church. Oh. I'm doing my bread. (*Mrs. Shandig crosses to kitchen table and begins to knead the dough.*)

## THE KITCHEN

(*Nun hesitates, then follows to* R. *of Mrs. Shandig.*)

NUN. When did all that happen?

MRS. SHANDIG. Two and a half years ago. When I came to Solon. I was married before. Oh no, I forgot about his egg nog.

NUN. Here I'll do that for you. (*Nun crosses around Mrs. Shandig and sits in chair to make egg nog.*)

MRS. SHANDIG. (*Continuing kneading.*) Thank you, Sister. I never knew very much. Cooking and cleaning, just that. I always worked at a camp. Lumbering. Those men. You wouldn't know how they are, Sister. If I tell you, you wouldn't like me.

NUN. You know that isn't true.

MRS. SHANDIG. But the students are waiting for you.

NUN. I left Louise in charge. Right now you're more important, Mrs. Shandig.

MRS. SHANDIG. I am? Well, my husband, he did the hunting for them at the camp. He brought me those bleeding animals. As long as I can remember I had to skin them and cook their bloody

15

meat. Every day I hoped he wouldn't come back. I did. Sister. I even prayed he wouldn't come back. Finally, then he didn't come back. I thought it was my fault, but Father says it wasn't. I had to run away then. From those other men in the camp. Without him there, they changed to me. They started grabbing after me. Poking at me with their spoons. I can't tell you what happened. I told Father. I never saw a town until I saw Solon. I didn't. They told me down there that Father needed a housekeeper. I never knew there was Catholics before that. I didn't. Just God. I owe everything to Father, so I have to help as much as can be. I try to be the best Catholic I can for him, but it's harder. Me being only a convert.

NUN. They always told me that converts make the best Catholics. Did you know that? You can be proud of it. You made a choice. I never had a choice.

MRS. SHANDIG. Don't tell anyone I wasn't born Catholic. No one else knows.

NUN. Sometime you look through Father's Saints Book and count how many of the saints were converts. You'll see.

MRS. SHANDIG. I can't read yet. I just want to.

NUN. (*Handing her a book.*) Well, soon, Mrs. Shandig. Very soon. (*Nun exits* R. *Rivard rises to watch her go. Lawyer enters* L. *and sits at desk with Rivard. Prosecutor and Secretary enter* L., *and go to witness stand.*)

## THE COURT

PROSECUTOR. At the time of the murder of Sister Rita, you were chief administrator of the Michigan diocese of the Holy Roman Church.

SECRETARY. I was and am Bishop Ginter's secretary. A position of greater responsibility than the title suggests. (*Mrs. Shandig exits* L., *taking kitchen props with her. Lawyer indicates to Rivard to sit down.*)

PROSECUTOR. Did you visit the defendant in his cell this morning?

SECRETARY. I did.

PROSECUTOR. What was the purpose of your meeting this morning?

SECRETARY. I offered to hear Confession.

PROSECUTOR. Did he accept the sacrament?

LAWYER. (*Rising, crossing toward Prosecutor.*) Objection. The Prosecution is attempting to seek—what do you call it?—privileged communication between the clergyman and the penitent.

PROSECUTOR. Privileged communication.

LAWYER. . . . Privileged communication between the clergyman and the, ah, penitent. (*Lawyer crosses to sit on desk.*)

PROSECUTOR. (*Crossing to lean on witness chair.*) I wouldn't seek privileged communication. I repeat, did the defendant confess?

SECRETARY. No. He is no longer a practicing Catholic. (*Prosecutor and Secretary now freeze in position as light goes to half on them.*)

LAWYER. I talked to Maurice about the last night. He did do the chore for you up at the Church, but he didn't see Sister Rita.

RIVARD. But he must have.

LAWYER. He'll swear under oath he didn't. (*Standing.*) I'm asking the sheriff to see if he can locate your Mrs. Shandig, so don't be discouraged. I'll think of something. (*Lawyer exits R. as Mrs. Shandig enters U. L. with egg nog.*)

## THE STUDY

MRS. SHANDIG. Father. Are you all right? (*Placing egg nog on desk, waiting for recognition.*) Father, if I'm disturbing you, tell me, and I'll just—

PRIEST. (*Continuing desk work.*) No. I'm glad you're here. I am.

MRS. SHANDIG. (*Pushing egg nog across desk.*) Here. It's time for your egg nog.

PRIEST. Thank you. You're determined to fatten me up, aren't you?

MRS. SHANDIG. Oh Father, go on with you. (*Indicating he should drink, then crossing D. R. to "open" a window. Sound of dog barking.*) We all have to keep up our health with the other nuns so sickly. Can I ask you something, Father?

PRIEST. (*Indicating for her to sit R. of desk.*) Of course, you can.

MRS. SHANDIG. It's personal and I don't want to be prying, Father. I don't. Too thick don't mix, I always say.

PRIEST. (*Sitting on D. edge of desk.*) Now come on, Mrs. Shandig. (*Again indicating where she may sit.*)

MRS. SHANDIG. (*Sitting, then after a moment.*) You've seemed so bothered.

PRIEST. Of course, I'm bothered. I have a great many things to worry about. (*Rising, pacing.*) What do they expect of me? The Bishop wants me to write this book, which anyone knows is a nearly impossible task. Then they expect me to turn the buttons from the collection plate into food for five mouths, to baptize a county full of Protestants, and to get my six very poor farmers to find the time to build a second outhouse so that the boys and girls can have recess at the same time. (*Stopping* D. R. *of* C.) And now on top of it all you expect me to drink the richest most repulsive concoction since—

MRS. SHANDIG. (*Rising, taking glass from his hand.*) You don't have to drink it. I'm only trying to help. (*She starts to exit.*)

PRIEST. I realize that. I'm sorry. (*He holds out hand for drink.*)

MRS. SHANDIG. Only if you want it.

PRIEST. I do. (*She hands it to him with pleasure. Priest drinks it in one swallow.*)

MRS. SHANDIG. Well, I guess it's best you say those things to me. Just so you don't have to talk out loud to yourself in the study.

PRIEST. You can hear me?

MRS. SHANDIG. Just a bit. Sometimes. I never understand about your writing problems, but if you talked with someone. . . .

PRIEST. (*Crossing* D. R. *to window.*) Maybe if I could talk it out. . . . Then maybe it would clarify. You know who I could discuss my book with?

MRS. SHANDIG. (*Following to "window."*) Sister.

PRIEST. (*Laughing.*) Yes. She's worked out well, hasn't she? School was over half an hour ago, and there's still a batch of them over there talking to her. It might be nice if I invited her over for supper some night.

MRS. SHANDIG. You'd be alone with a nun, Father.

PRIEST. Well, believe it or not, Mrs. Shandig, I am capable of remarkable propriety.

MRS. SHANDIG. I know that. Why Father, everyone thinks you are the finest person that ever they knew.

PRIEST. And well they should, shouldn't they?

MRS. SHANDIG. I think so.

PRIEST. I care about other people, don't I?

MRS. SHANDIG. Yes, you do, Father.

PRIEST. Like Sister. With the other nuns ill. Sister has no one to eat with, and therefore—

MRS. SHANDIG. Father, you know nuns expect to be lonely.

PRIEST. No. No one expects that. (*Crossing up to desk.*) Why should the Church cause loneliness? That's what I don't understand. Loneliness is not contagious, you know, yet people stand by and willingly watch others suffer as if they were afraid they'll catch it by intervening. It makes me wonder if we are naturally cruel. Something, here, inside, makes us, unlike God, revel in misery. (*Sister Rita enters around* u. *footstool to* u. *of stage.*)

NUN. I hope I'm not interrupting. The children and I just had a wonderful idea. (*Silence.*) What is wrong?

PRIEST. Shouldn't you have sent a note, Sister?

NUN. We just thought of it.

PRIEST. The other nuns always ask to see me first.

MRS. SHANDIG. Sister, it's only for the students. They'll be thinking it is all right to come running over here whenever they want.

NUN. (*Starting to exit.*) Father. I'm sorry.

PRIEST. Actually I don't mind. I'm like you and tend to be too pragmatic forgetting there may be excellent reasons for traditions that are momentarily troublesome as Mrs. Shandig was just reminding me. Now what have you and the students thought up?

NUN. Painting.

MRS. SHANDIG. What would they paint, Sister?

PRIEST. The cloakroom is covered with little handprints. A darker—

NUN. No. Pictures. Flowers, trees. Their houses.

PRIEST. (*Motioning Nun to sit* L.) That's good, Sister. I like it.

NUN. (*Sitting.*) Thank you, Father.

PRIEST. (*Sitting* R.) The lives of the saints would make good subjects, and at Christmas they could—

NUN. We can even add it to the curriculum.

PRIEST. We don't have to do that. I'd have to ask the Bishop.

NUN. Tell him our problem. I've never seen children with so little sense of what is good in life. So little imagination.

PRIEST. (*Rising, crossing around desk* u.) Yes. I like the idea. Now we'll need paper.

NUN. There's plenty of composition paper, Father.

PRIEST. Now your imagination is wanting. Their world's got to be bigger than composition paper. Would it matter if the paper were tan?

NUN. Why?

PRIEST. There's a butcher in Traverse City who's Catholic.

MRS. SHANDIG. Bernard Christiansen.

PRIEST. When I take the other nuns in to the doctor, I'll pay that butcher a visit.

MRS. SHANDIG. What about paints?

NUN. Maybe when you write the Bishop, he could send—

PRIEST. But I'd rather not write the Bishop.

MRS. SHANDIG. I have the Sears and Roebuck Catalog in my room.

PRIEST. Good. We'll try that.

NUN. (*Rising, crossing to* R.) I could write the Bishop. He's very proud of me because—

PRIEST. No. I don't want you to. You might end up in as much difficulty as I am.

MRS. SHANDIG. (*Crossing* u. *of desk.*) What difficulty?

NUN. What do you mean?

PRIEST. Well, nothing really important I suppose.

NUN. (*Sitting.*) Well, I wouldn't care what they did to me, Father. I wouldn't feel right having the children paint during school time unless it was part of the curriculum.

MRS. SHANDIG. What difficulty are you talking about? (*She sits on* u. *stool as lights come up on court.*)

## THE COURT

PROSECUTOR. (*Turning back* D.) I understand that there had been no priest assigned to Solon for nearly a decade prior to Father Rivard.

SECRETARY. Nine years.

PROSECUTOR. Why was such a change made?

SECRETARY. Father Rivard's particular talents seemed more useful up here.

PROSECUTOR. Was he sent to this out-of-the-way post because he was a troublemaker?

SECRETARY. Father Rivard was incredibly energetic and popular with parishioners and therefore a bit of an aggravation to the

20

senior priests wherever we put him. The Bishop thought by bringing him into the Chancery he might personally be able to guide the young priest. But Father Rivard did not readily accede to such help. The Bishop had to request me to stop Father Rivard from entering his office without an appointment. He would burst in and no matter who was present bring up an obscure theological point, suggest his ideas for raising funds through games of chance as is done in certain eastern cities . . . And there was ultimately an incident of his usurping a responsibility that was distinctly the privilege of Bishop Ginter. (*Prosecutor exits* U. L. *A Gregorian chant can be heard distantly.*)

## THE CHANCERY

PRIEST. (*Standing.*) You told me to look in on Mother Vincent.

SECRETARY. (*Rising.*) But not to give Last Rites. You knew the Bishop was available. (*They walk together to cell.*)

PRIEST. She asked me to. She told me to. She was so feverish that she was nearly mad.

SECRETARY. She asked, did she?

PRIEST. Yes.

SECRETARY. Of course, you assume there would be no way for me to confirm that.

PRIEST. We were alone.

SECRETARY. (*Sitting on* R. *stool.*) Mother Vincent did not die.

PRIEST. Oh, I'm so glad. No one told me. Will she be—

SECRETARY. And she remembers nothing of requesting Last Rites. In fact—

PRIEST. Well, she was delirious and—

SECRETARY. Enough. You are to be assigned immediately to a parish far from the Chancery. (*Silence.*)

PRIEST. (*Sitting on* L. *stool.*) You would punish me for being compassionate.

SECRETARY. Is that the way you see it?

PRIEST. I know Bishop Ginter would not—

SECRETARY. Father Rivard, I hardly think I need remind you again that I speak for the Bishop.

PRIEST. (*Rising.*) When a priest is asked to give the Sacrament, he is bound to give it; she begged me. Did you want me to get a medical opinion? By that time she could have been dead.

21

SECRETARY. The Bishop assumes you've read St. Augustine. *Confessiones? De Civitate Dei?*

PRIEST. Of course.

SECRETARY. Have you read *De Fide Vero?*

PRIEST. *Of True Religion.*

SECRETARY. I didn't think a translation necessary. (*Indicating Priest should again sit which he does.*) When still a young man, about your age I would say, Aurelius Augustinius, long before he was Bishop of Hippo, before he even thought of being consecrated Bishop . . . he went into a five-year period of seclusion while he wrote many philosophical studies. It tuned his mind, disciplined his spirit and prepared him for the robes you are so eager to don. And so you shall. Read . . . *Of True Religion* closely, carefully. Then write your concept of the Church's authority. When your study is completed, in a couple of years I would say, I shall read it. When I have read it, the Bishop will read it. And we shall discuss your new understanding and future.

PRIEST. I won't do it.

SECRETARY. Why?

PRIEST. Priests are assigned according to the needs of the parish and the talents of—

SECRETARY. (*Standing, clearly angry.*) Enough. Questioning dogma. Then usurping the Bishop's responsibility. Now scattering Last Rites to the living like a housewife feeding fowl. (*A moment while he calms himself.*) I have located a parish that will suit your contemplative pursuits.

PRIEST. (*Standing.*) I am not a contemplative man. (*Secretary sits.*) You don't know me if you'd waste the good I'm capable of.

SECRETARY. Of which you are capable. The Indian name for Solon was Land of Rainbows. Attractive, peaceful. Perfect for the seclusion St. Augustine similarly sought in his preparation for becoming a Bishop.

PRIEST. I won't go until I speak to the Bishop.

SECRETARY. (*Standing.*) He is consecrating a church in Saginaw. He left you a letter. (*Music fades as Priest kneels and Secretary makes sign of cross over him.*) He wishes you God's speed.

## THE STUDY

(*Lights come up on Study area.*)

NUN. One reason. Just one reason I can understand why you

won't write the Bishop for permission for painting. That's all I ask.

PRIEST. (*Crossing to desk, sitting.*) Well, maybe I've gotten a bit gun-shy, Sister. What do you think?

NUN. We could all say a prayer that the Bishop will fill your request, Father. (*She stands. Priest smiles. Monsignor exits* R. *as Nun exits* L., *calling to children.*) Children. Father said yes. He'll hear from the Bishop in just a few . . .

## THE CELL

LAWYER. (*Crossing into cell* L.) What about this business I've heard tell that Sister Rita lived with you?

PRIEST. (*Crossing into cell* R.) She didn't live with me. It was an emergency measure. That's all. She stayed in the rectory. We seldom even ate together.

LAWYER. Then why didn't you tell me before? I've got two days. These circuit judges don't smile on long trials, Father. Don't withhold information from me.

RIVARD. It's not important.

LAWYER. That prosecutor can build his whole case on this. He's good. He's young. At the rate he's going, why with cases like this, he'll be writing laws in Lansing before he's thirty-five. With a motive like that, the jury won't hesitate to hang you. This is exactly the kind of thing Protestants are sure happens behind those heavy lace curtains in rectories. If there is one thing they hate more than Catholics out here, it's sex. (*Sitting on* R. *stool.*) Why did you take her out of the convent and into the house with you?

RIVARD. The other sisters had consumption. They could not be moved.

LAWYER. Couldn't you send her to another convent? (*Nun enters* R. *and remains* L. *of Rivard.*)

RIVARD. I was afraid we'd have to close the school.

NUN. Father, I can't believe you'd even think of closing the school.

LAWYER. Why would you have to close the school? I don't understand.

RIVARD. I couldn't teach all the classes.

NUN. Mrs. Shandig said I have to leave because—

LAWYER. But you taught before the nuns came.

NUN. Not all by yourself. We could share the teaching and keep the school open.

LAWYER. Why did she have to live in the rectory of all places? Come on, Rivard. You said you're strong enough. For God's sake, give me some help. (*Rivard turns away from Lawyer.*)

RIVARD. The doctor said she couldn't live under the same roof with two consumptives. (*Lawyer exits* L.)

NUN. There are rooms to rent above Maurice's blacksmith shop.

## THE CLASSROOM

PRIEST. (*Standing.*) It would be too dangerous. Last year they broke into Widow Webber's house and—

NUN. Then up here. The rectory. Your house.

PRIEST. (*Crossing* U. L. *to table.*) Your community wouldn't allow it. Sister, we have Holy Laws to guide us.

NUN. (*Crossing* L. *of table.*) I believe the Church stands for people, not Laws. If you wrote Mother Vincent, she'd realize—

PRIEST. (*Sitting on edge of table.*) I wish I could. Priests don't deal with the Mother House. Only the Bishop.

NUN. Ask him for a dispensation. Then Mother Vincent would have to—

PRIEST. Sister, this is not easy, but it must be. It must be.

NUN. Very little must be, Father. Please. God knows everything we do is for the Church. He knows we do it for the sake of His children. (*Showing Priest students' drawings.*) They are responding, learning from me. They need me, Father. It could be months before there'd be another teaching assignment for me again. (*Calming down as Priest shows interest in drawings.*) I don't think they believe I'm a very good teacher. They didn't really want to send me up here, but I have been good. Haven't I?

PRIEST. (*Standing.*) This is not a personal question. I built the school. I want it open.

NUN. But this is my responsibility.

PRIEST. Your spiritual guidance, your life in Christ is my responsibility.

NUN. And what about your responsibility to the children.

PRIEST. You want to break the laws for yourself, not the children. You feel useful. That's the sin of pride.

24

NUN. And you? Keeping the school open all by yourself. How good would that be for the children.

PRIEST. I am trying to do the best I can, Sister. I cannot do more.

NUN. What have I done wrong? Why do you want me to leave?

PRIEST. I didn't say I want you to leave. This is not a personal question. Why do you always insist upon making everything a personal question. (*Mrs. Shandig enters* R.)

## THE STUDY

MRS. SHANDIG. The letter's here. From the Bishop, Father. He won't let Sister move in here. (*Rivard crosses to desk, sits, opens letter.*) I'm certain of it. I don't know why you even asked him.

PRIEST. (*Reading letter.*) Mrs. Shandig, he gave permission for you to live here.

MRS. SHANDIG. But I'm not a nun. I'm not. That makes all the difference. (*Priest finishes reading. Silence. Mrs. Shandig sits.*) What did he tell you, Father?

PRIEST. He doesn't want me to close the school.

MRS. SHANDIG. But Sister. What does he say about Sister?

PRIEST. Nothing. He didn't mention her.

MRS. SHANDIG. No. He had to. He told you she can't live here, didn't he?

PRIEST. "I am stunned to read that you considered suspending classes at the very time our Diocese is enjoying the most rapid rate of expansion of any in America. Your fine record cannot but reassure me that you have already resolved your local administrative problem without further need of advice from me. I am certain you are finding staying in the village uncomfortable, but it will surely not be for long." The Bishop didn't answer me. It's Monsignor, that hypocrite. (*Priest rips letter, throws pieces on floor.*)

MRS. SHANDIG. (*Kneels to pick up letter.*) Father, what's wrong. You mustn't talk so.

PRIEST. (*Kneeling to talk with her.*) You hear what he wants. He wants me to live in town. To leave four women defenseless on this hill.

MRS. SHANDIG. No. You can't live down there. Those men are vicious. They're vicious, Father. I go down every day. I know.

NUN. (*From classroom.*) Do you want me to leave?

PRIEST. Do you want Sister to live down there?

MRS. SHANDIG. No, Father.

NUN. Everything we do is for the Church. (*Nun exits* L.)

PRIEST. (*Rises, crosses* U.) Here then. My house. I'll go and tell her.

MRS. SHANDIG. Father, no. The Church has a rule so we—

PRIEST. I know Church law only too well, certainly better than you, and I don't require your services to remind me.

MRS. SHANDIG. Oh, Father. Father. Why do you talk like this? I only want to help. It's wrong for Sister to move in here. I just know it.

PRIEST. (*Crossing* U. R. *of Mrs. Shandig, around desk.*) I believe it is the Will of God that we keep the school open. I'm sorry if your interpretation is different from mine.

MRS. SHANDIG. (*Suddenly crying.*) Oh, Father. Please I'm trying. I don't know what to do for you anymore. I just want to be so good for you.

PRIEST. No more now. No crying. Everything will be all right.

GUARD'S VOICE. The Prosecution calls Miss Louise Donnelly for the People. (*Louise and Prosecutor enter* U. L. *Lawyer enters* R. *Mrs. Shandig exits* R.)

## THE COURT

(*Louise, a college girl with all the liberation and pretension of half an education, is on the stand. Lawyer sits on* R. *chair. Rivard sits on* L. *chair.*)

PROSECUTOR. Did you know Sister Rita well, Louise?

LOUISE. Yes. As a matter of fact, it was she who first suggested I had the potentiality for college. No girl from Solon would ever have thought of such a thing. I have just completed one semester at Central Normal. I am, in a sense, indebted to Sister Rita. She had flaws, I suppose, being a nun and all. But she always took time to—

PROSECUTOR. Did you know Father Rivard? (*Mrs. Shandig enters* R. *with dinner props.*)

LOUISE. Yes.

PROSECUTOR. How would you describe him? (*Nun enters* L.)

LOUISE. We liked him. That is, until Sister moved into the rectory. After that, in cathechism.

PROSECUTOR. She moved in with the priest . . . (*Mrs. Shandig puts tray on table. Rivard and Shandig move table* D. C., *bring chairs.*)

LOUISE. I remember the day. It was like a holiday. All Sister did was lead games and teach songs. That night she moved into his house. By the next morning everyone knew she was living in the rectory with him.

## THE DINING ROOM

(*Mrs. Shandig is setting table as Nun enters with flowers.*)

NUN. (*Standing* U. *of table.*) Rather a sad offering I'm afraid. But this is my first evening, my first dinner . . . I wanted to bring you something. Are there any flowers up here in the summer? I saw you planting your garden, Mrs. Shandig, but you only planted vegetables. (*Mrs. Shandig is about to comment negatively.*)

PRIEST. You're right. That's what's missing up here. Flowers. I suppose I could transplant some lilacs up from the valley. But they wouldn't have much of a chance if I did. I don't have the knack for making things grow. They are usually green for the exact length of time they take to die.

NUN. (*Crossing* D. L. *to look out window.*) Listen, if you'll get the lilac, I could start a garden down the hill a bit, and then they'll see flowers when they look up at Holy Rosary. I haven't had a garden since I was fourteen, when they took me to Guardian Angel. (*Mrs. Shandig exits* L. *Silence.*)

PRIEST. (*Awkwardly.*) How are Sister Martha and Sister Immaculata tonight?

NUN. They feel well enough to envy me moving here. Especially Sister Martha. She's the clever one, you know. She was joking. (*Silence.*)

PRIEST. It will be cool after dinner so I thought we might have dessert in my study. I laid the fire with birch. (*He indicates she may sit.*)

NUN. That's very thoughtful, Father. Thank you.

PRIEST. (*Realizing he should hold chair, hurries to her.*) Sometimes it's good to plan ahead, to look forward a bit. (*He awkwardly indicates she may sit, pushes chair in too hard, sits down himself. Silence.*)

NUN. Planning ahead can be the best part sometimes, though,

27

don't you think, Father? (*Silence.*) I saw Governor Pingree once. We planned it for two months. A group of novices went on the train to Lansing. The Fourth of July. When my aunt came to visit me later, she looked at my postal cards. And for once I could tell my aunt things . . .

PRIEST. Didn't your aunt like to talk with you?

NUN. Well, I think communicating is very important. For me conversation is as essential as breathing.

PRIEST. I've noticed.

NUN. But my aunt. I loved her, Father, but I wasn't her niece. Not really. She was paid to keep, take care of me. Her husband had an accident in the barn with the horse. He was in bed without ever waking up for several days before he died. My aunt, she blamed me. She said the accident was my fault. I was playing up in the loft and . . . in a way it was. I had to sit by his bed then. I was so scared. I didn't know what was to become of me if he died. I watched a sparrow in the garden, and he made me laugh. My aunt heard me laughing. It made her so mad that she said terrible, cruel . . . that nobody loved me or would ever love me. She said no one would ever even talk with me after what I'd— I don't know exactly what happened. There were days then . . . well, they said the priest, Father Walling, could hear me when he came and made her unlock me. He took me away, to Guardian Angel Convent, and the good sisters watched over me. (*Silence.*) That's what you meant. The first day. Not thinking of the past. (*Silence.*)

PRIEST. (*Crossing u. to call.*) Maybe Mrs. Shandig has forgotten we're here. Mrs. Shandig, we're ready to eat. It's a stew. I always sample what she's cooking in the afternoon. It's good. (*He returns to seat.*)

NUN. Since Mrs. Shandig has Thursdays for her day off, I thought you might like it if I cooked for us.

PRIEST. That would be splendid. But only if you'll have the time. (*Mrs. Shandig has entered.*)

NUN. I'll have time. If I'm going to live here, I want to do my share. And that should make it a bit easier on you, Mrs. Shandig. (*Silence.*) Is there a little jug, Mrs. Shandig? We could put some water in it, and the flowers might be pretty on the—

MRS. SHANDIG. We don't have anything the right size, Sister.

NUN. Even a glass would be— (*Mrs. Shandig moves to exit.*)

PRIEST. Mrs. Shandig. Please bring me a glass for them. I haven't

28

seen flowers where I lived since I was a young man. I'd like it. Put them in my study, and you can put one of your doilies under it.

MRS. SHANDIG. Yes, Father. (*Mrs. Shandig exits* U. L.)

NUN. I think I must have hurt Mrs. Shandig somehow. Maybe in her reading lesson.

PRIEST. She likes flowers, I think.

NUN. Well, have I offended her? I'd apologize.

NUN *and* PRIEST. (*Praying.*) Bless us, oh Lord, and these Thy gifts which we are about to receive from Thy bounty through Christ our Lord. Amen.

PRIEST. No. It was me. I offended her. Mrs. Shandig thinks I should not eat with you. She thinks there would be . . . ramifications.

NUN. But there are none. Mrs. Shandig is in the house. This is exactly what Sister Martha was teasing me about.

PRIEST. People always want to think the worst. I remember when I was a young man, in my teens actually, I fell terribly and instantly in love with a merchant's daughter who wore blonde sausage curls. It's quite true. No nice girl in our town had ever dared to wear sausage curls, but this girl was from a good family and she did. It all would have come to naught except she found my eyelashes to be a "marvel of the modern world." Those were her words I'm afraid. Every now and again I see my eyelashes in a looking glass, and still I don't understand her fascination. But it was real enough for her, and we were inseparable, even thinking it would be romantic if we could convince the priest to let us make confession together. Everyone expected the worst would happen to us. My uncle, two cousins, our priest and the barber, all told me in increasing detail what a girl with sausage curls would expect of me, and how it would ruin my life. They would not relent. They fussed and tore at me like dogs with a knotted sock. Things I never knew the name of before then became everyday threats, hourly horrors finally. I couldn't think of anything but what they expected. Then she was sent away. Humiliated in front of everyone, and it was my— There. I'm talking of the past. (*He stands.*)

NUN. Don't be unrealistic in what you expect of yourself, Father. Everyone thinks of the past. It's natural.

PRIEST. I think it's the Baptists, they stand up and tell what sins they committed before being saved. I've always thought that if I

29

did that, if people knew what I was, how I thought before I entered the priesthood, people would either reject me outright or they would know how essential the Church is for a decent life. The Church is the most beautiful institution of which I can conceive. A wonder, like the greatest work of art. Perfectly logical and divine. Making absolute order from absolute chaos. The Church makes my life, and life possible. *Yet* during the past winter here with these slow country people, the sisters both sick, it seemed as though—well, I weakened. I wondered if the Church were as perfect as I believed. Then you came, with your vitality, your joy in the Church, and all my enthusiasm returned. But now, people are talking about you moving in here. (*Priest takes Nun's hand.*) It's like a cloud settling on us. Sometimes, sometimes I nearly despair there will ever be justice in people.

NUN. (*Putting other hand on Priest's which holds hers.*) We don't always see it, I know, but God is just. And we couldn't know God if justice weren't in us. (*Priest withdraws hand as he realizes what has happened.*)

PRIEST. This, Sister, this now, is exactly why people think nuns and priests should not be alone together.

NUN. I don't know—

PRIEST. This kind of informal conversation encourages what I feared would—encourages a lack of discipline. (*Pause.*) We, we won't be able to take our meals together.

NUN. But, Father, when we talk, everything seems all right.

PRIEST. What does that mean?

NUN. Like I'm a person. I am so weary of hearing Sister's rosary, Sister's book, Sister's this, Sister's that. Never just hers.

PRIEST. It is not for us to worry how we are feeling. We must be separate from the world. All that chaos.

NUN. God isn't separate. Not from the world. Not from the things people do and feel. He came to earth as a baby. He worked as a carpenter, drank wine, loved the children. We are like God. You can't make God into something else than what you already know. If you do, then you're making God into your image. And God made us in—

PRIEST. (*Angry.*) Sister. (*Smiling.*) Oh, Sister, do you know, you sound very much like a Protestant? (*Priest sits at table with Nun to watch trial.*)

PROSECUTOR. Were there any other unusual changes after Sister started living with the priest? (*Mrs. Shandig enters* L. *Nun and Shandig move table to original place and clean it off. They then exit* R.)

LOUISE. Sophie . . . she was another student . . . Sophie and I, we had a great fiction between us that the priest and Sister were in love. We even talked—

PROSECUTOR. Did I hear right? "In love"?

LAWYER. (*Standing.*) Objection. The testimony reads: "Sophie and I had a great fiction . . ."

PROSECUTOR. What gave rise to this fiction?

LOUISE. Well, for example . . . When we went into town, Sister would watch him through the window riding down, while she taught. He was, still is, a very attractive man.

LAWYER. Mr. Rivard's appeal to the witness has never been in question.

PROSECUTOR. (*Crouches beside witness chair.*) Did you ever confront either the sister or the priest with your opinions, Louise?

LOUISE. Yes. Sophie dared me to ask Sister Rita why priest and nuns couldn't marry. (*Prosecutor and Lawyer stand* L.)

## THE STUDY

PRIEST. (*Standing, crossing to Louise as he speaks.*) Sister tells me you are full of questions these days, Louise.

LOUISE. (*Standing.*) So is Sophie.

PRIEST. I didn't ask to see you so I could punish you. (*Louise begins cross to follow Priest into Study.*)

LOUISE. Then why?

PRIEST. To see if I can't answer some of your questions. Sit down. (*Moving chair to front of desk for her, sitting on edge of desk.*) I thought it might be nice for us to have a conversation.

LOUISE. Your house is nice, Father.

PRIEST. Thank you. (*Silence.*)

LOUISE. Sister Rita's nice.

PRIEST. A good teacher.

LOUISE. Better than Sister Immaculata. She's crabby.

PRIEST. She's not well you know.

LOUISE. Do you think Sister Rita is nice, Father?

PRIEST. Yes.

LOUISE. How much?

PRIEST. What do you mean?

LOUISE. I like her a lot.

PRIEST. You should.

LOUISE. Do you?

PRIEST. How much do you think about this?

LOUISE. What?

PRIEST. Sister and I.

LOUISE. Never.

PRIEST. Lies are venial sins, Louise.

LOUISE. I thought you liked me.

PRIEST. That's why I want to help you.

LOUISE. You don't like me.

PRIEST. Louise. I like you. All right?

LOUISE. If you did you'd tell me things.

PRIEST. What things?

LOUISE. Things.

PRIEST. It is very hard to carry on a conversation with you, Louise.

LOUISE. What if someone loved you?

PRIEST. I see.

LOUISE. Priests love everyone, don't they?

PRIEST. Yes. Everyone. And that's not love to marry by. Love between a man and a woman isn't controlled by ideals as it is when you say you love people, everyone. Understand?

LOUISE. No.

PRIEST. Love between a man and woman is unordered.

LOUISE. Families are ordered.

PRIEST. Married love is totally consuming. It takes time, frustration and a great deal of effort. Now that I think of it, I wonder that anyone goes to the trouble.

LOUISE. Oh, I know why.

PRIEST. I doubt you do.

LOUISE. I understand things so well when you explain them. I love your devotions.

PRIEST. Thank you.

LOUISE. So tell me, Father.

PRIEST. What? (*Mrs. Shandig enters with two egg nogs* R.)

LOUISE. What would you do if someone said they loved you?

PRIEST. Sister Rita and I have to be clear-headed to help people, Louise. How could we be married, worried about each other, bothered about ice bills and the children's teeth?

LOUISE. I didn't mean Sister Rita. What would you say? (*Silence as Priest stands, walks to his desk chair and sits.*)

PRIEST. There are things, young lady, that are a sin even to think about, let alone say. One has to discipline one's mind as well as actions. And you remember that. To think something is as great a sin as to do it. (*Mrs. Shandig brings two egg nogs to desk.*)

LOUISE. (*To Mrs. Shandig.*) Thank you. There aren't raw eggs in this, are there?

MRS. SHANDIG. It's good for you.

LOUISE. Ich. I hate raw eggs. Can I go?

PRIEST. Of course.

LOUISE. Bye. (*Louise exits to witness stand.*)

MRS. SHANDIG. (*As she exits with glasses.*) There are some ideas she has there, Father.

PRIEST. Yes, aren't they.

## THE COURT

PROSECUTOR. Do you think you could have imagined there was a romance because being such an obviously aware, intelligent child, you did observe precisely the telling details which could lead to the only possible logical conclusion?

LOUISE. The priest was having carnal knowledge of the nun.

LAWYER. (*Laughing.*) That's not the only conclusion. It's certainly not a possible conclusion. And it is not a logical conclusion. I don't even think it is a conclusion.

PROSECUTOR. (*Crossing* u. l.) I withdraw the question. Your witness.

LAWYER. (*Standing, crossing to witness.*) Now, Louise. Did you ever imagine the priest in bed?

LOUISE. I don't know. Probably I did.

LAWYER. Who was in bed with the priest in your fantasies? Who did you imagine?

LOUISE. I guess Sister Rita.

LAWYER. Now, Louise, what do you guess you imagined them doing?

LOUISE. I didn't know then about . . . such things.

LAWYER. You didn't.

LOUISE. Just, well, sounds. I imagined sounds. That's all.

LAWYER. Did you ever imagine someone other than Sister Rita. Up there. In bed. With the priest. Making sounds? Anyone at all? (*Silence.*) Did you confess your fantasies to the priest? (*Rivard crosses to* U. L. *of cell.*)

LOUISE. He was most cruel and extreme in his penance.

LAWYER. Extreme?

LOUISE. Especially after the Monsignor visited.

LAWYER. He was even stricter after the Monsignor visited. (*Secretary enters up ramp.*)

LOUISE. He forbade me having lunch with the other children and instead made me say endless Hail Marys and Our Fathers during recess. You can't imagine the ridicule to which I was subjected. I was a sensitive child. I begged him to relent, but not him.

LAWYER. It would be nice to get even, wouldn't it, Louise? (*Prosecutor is about to object, but Lawyer is quicker.*) No further questions. (*Lawyer, Prosecutor, Louise exit* L.)


## THE STUDY

SECRETARY. Father Rivard. (*Rivard turns to greet Secretary.*) After your extraordinary request, a Sister of Mercy living in the rectory, I thought it best I visit. I am most curious to discover why your question was ever asked.

PRIEST. But to come so far, and not even to let us prepare—

SECRETARY. Not far. The Bishop will consecrate the parish hall in Traverse City tonight. I have but one hour here. First, the Bishop wishes I speak with Sister Rita. Will you send your cook to the convent for her? (*Mrs. Shandig enters, holds hand up against sun, trying to see down the hill, then kneels* L. *and begins to weed her garden.*)

PRIEST. But, Monsignor, you see—

SECRETARY. Ah, Sister's teaching.

PRIEST. Yes, the school. She might be there.

SECRETARY. Then someone will watch her class. (*Nun entrs* L. *and begins to help Mrs. Shandig in garden.*)

PRIEST. There's no classes on Saturday.

SECRETARY. Do you want me not to see Sister, Father Rivard?

PRIEST. Oh no. (*Realizing Secretary is still standing on front porch.*) Come in, Monsignor. I'll go myself. (*They cross to desk.*)

SECRETARY. (*Sitting* L.) Perhaps there is something I might be reading in the meantime. For company.

PRIEST. (*Crossing* U. R. *of desk.*) I've finished three chapters.

SECRETARY. How many will there be, Father?

PRIEST. Seven.

SECRETARY. I see. One for each of the deadly sins.

PRIEST. Yes. Monday, Tuesday, Wednesday—

SECRETARY. Am I to take it that this parish is not to your liking?

PRIEST. You'll see that the other four chapters are outlined in detail. (*Priest exits toward garden, then paces* U. L. *as he tries to figure out what to do.*)

## MRS. SHANDIG'S KITCHEN GARDEN

MRS. SHANDIG. Is someone visiting Father?

NUN. Everyone was here for Confession this morning.

MRS. SHANDIG. It's that sun. All but makes you see things.

NUN. Imagine how it will be on the farms come harvest. They can't possibly carry water to the fields, just our gardens are more than enough to do.

MRS. SHANDIG. Sister. Those aren't weeds. They're new radishes.

NUN. I'm sorry.

MRS. SHANDIG. Sister. I never wanted you to move in because of the rule, but I like having you at the rectory. I do.

NUN. I do too, Mrs. Shandig. (*Priest crosses* D. R. *of Nun.*)

PRIEST. Sister, I have got to talk to you. Monsignor Nicholson is here.

NUN. (*Standing.*) Right here in Solon.

PRIEST. In my study.

MRS. SHANDIG. (*Starting to exit* L.) Oh no. Not when it looks so— I haven't dusted since Tuesday.

PRIEST. I'd rather he not know that Sister lives in the rectory.

NUN. Doesn't he know already?

MRS. SHANDIG. Do you mean I should lie?

PRIEST. (*Crossing toward Mrs. Shandig.*) No. Not that. But, everything short of lying. He, this Monsignor Nicholson, he, he's

35

always looking for some mistake, some infringement, some mere interpretation that would prove that I am not capable to—
MRS. SHANDIG. (*Exiting* L.) Father, I'll help.
PRIEST. Come on then.

## THE STUDY

(*Priest and Nun cross to study.*)
SECRATARY. (*Closing manuscript.*) Pithy. Pithy, Father. Far more than I expected.
PRIEST. Why?
SECRETARY. (*Standing.*) Sister Rita. The Bishop sends you greetings.
NUN. Thank you, Monsignor.
SECRETARY. (*Indicating Nun is to sit.*) He is concerned for your well-being, Sister.
NUN. (*Sitting.*) When the doctor comes to see the sister, he talks with all of us. (*Mrs. Shandig enters with tea tray from* L.)
SECRETARY. He wonders if we shouldn't consider closing the school, if it isn't—
NUN. But, Father worked so hard to build it and—
SECRETARY. Yes. Yes. But until any danger of consumption—
NUN. There's none. I'm not exposed to them.
SECRETARY. You're not? (*Priest picks up manuscript as Mrs. Shandig puts tray on desk.*)
MRS. SHANDIG. Sister doesn't sleep in the same room with them.
SECRETARY. You're the cook.
PRIEST. Mrs. Shandig. Monsignor.
SECRETARY. Yes. Where do you sleep, Sister?
MRS. SHANDIG. Sugar, Monsignor?
SECRETARY. Sister, I asked where you sleep since the other sisters—
NUN. Of course, I see them for prayers, but we are careful.
PRIEST. No sugar for me.
SECRETARY. Sister.
NUN. (*Starting simultaneously with Priest.*) I go to Mass in the Church. They take the Sacrament—
PRIEST. Have you any thoughts on my progress with the book? (*Mrs. Shandig hands Secretary tea cup.*)

36

SECRETARY. No. And I don't have time for tea. Sister. I asked you a question.

PRIEST. At least, tell me, does the book look to be acceptable?

SECRETARY. Are you all hiding something from me? (*Silence.*)

NUN. I sleep in the Convent of course. (*Looking to Priest for approval, then standing.*) Will you come and see the school before you leave?

SECRETARY. Certainly. Thank you, Sister.

NUN. (*As they exit* u. l.) We are terribly pleased with what the children have accomplished. (*As soon as Nun and Secretary have exited* l., *Priest throws manuscript on floor.*)

PRIEST. What have I done? What have I done? (*Mrs. Shandig picks up manuscript, puts tea tray on stool as Nun enters, brings chair* u. *of table and sits to break string beans.*)

## THE KITCHEN

MRS. SHANDIG. (*Taking "reader" from apron and placing it on table in front of Nun.*) I've stopped reading lessons.

NUN. Why?

MRS. SHANDIG. I read good enough now for an older person. I'm not taking Thursdays off for a while. I'll do the cooking.

NUN. But that's the one day I cook. It gives you a little time for yourself.

MRS. SHANDIG. I just stay in my room, anyway. You cook too much, Sister.

NUN. Just Thursdays.

MRS. SHANDIG. No. Too much meat. I can't do anything with leftover meat on Friday.

NUN. (*Standing, taking off apron.*) Well, why didn't you tell me, Mrs. Shandig?

MRS. SHANDIG. (*Standing, beginning to string beans.*) I told Father.

NUN. He didn't tell me. He has not said a word to me the last week about anything.

MRS. SHANDIG. He broke my bowl.

NUN. What do you mean?

MRS. SHANDIG. My good one. The blue glass fruit bowl. On purpose.

NUN. Why, Mrs. Shandig?

37

MRS. SHANDIG. (*Crying.*) I don't know, Sister. Father's so strange. I'm worried. I told him about the leftover meat when you cook, and he banged the table so hard he knocked my bowl over.

NUN. What did he say about me? (*Priest enters, ignores Nun.*)

PRIEST. (*Crossing* R. *of table.*) Mrs. Shandig, I have to go over to Leland. I will not be back in time for dinner.

NUN. (*Crossing around Mrs. Shandig.*) Father, I could wait up and cook you some—

PRIEST. (*To Mrs. Shandig.*) I am speaking at the Grange. I believe they will serve supper there.

NUN. Why are you pretending that I'm not here?

PRIEST. Because as far as I am concerned you are not.

MRS. SHANDIG. (*Rising, moving to exit.*) Father, would you excuse me? I have to feed the—

PRIEST. (U. *of table.*) No. You stay. It was wrong of me to have Sister move in here. You were right, Mrs. Shandig. But I can't send Sister to Detroit now that she lied to Monsignor. They'd punish her so that—

NUN. But you were there. You could have corrected me, Father.

PRIEST. From now on, if you see me on the stairs, in the hall, anywhere, you will ignore it. As far as I am concerned you are back in the convent, and you will think the same. If it is ever necessary for me to speak to you, I will come to the school. (*Priest "exits" u. R. and picks up harness.*)

NUN. (*Calling after Priest.*) Father, I only lied to Monsignor so that you wouldn't. . . . (*Mrs. Shandig exits L.*

## THE PARLOR

NUN. (*Priest takes harness and a chair and sits R. Nun crosses D. R. and moves cell stools slightly U. to form a "window seat." She gets her scissors and brown paper. She waits in hopes Priest will speak. The wind outside and a ticking clock in the hall can be heard under scene. Nun crossing toward Priest.*) Father? A month. It's been a month since Monsignor visited. Four weeks, Father, and— (*Silence as Priest continues polishing harness with vigor. Nun sits on L. stool and watches Mrs. Shandig enter with bowl of apples. Mrs. Shandig pulls a chair D. C., slightly above Priest's. She offers him apple, which Priest refuses. Mrs. Shandig sits and begins paring apples. Nun is frustrated by silence, looks out window to valley,*

38

*fights back tears of frustration. She takes a chair from the study and brings it down and sits in front of "window seat." She begins to noisily cut a design in the brown wrapping paper. Eventually, the Priest throws down harness with annoyance. He takes missal from pocket and begins to read. Nun, catching a look from the Priest, tries to cut more quietly. Thereby making even more noise.)*

MRS. SHANDIG. *(Unable to bear tension in the room.)* What are you making?

NUN. Oh, for the school. Flowers. *(She holds up design.)* I thought the younger children could paint them bright colors, and Louise could put them up with the compositions.

MRS. SHANDIG. *(Worried about Priest, trying to stop conversation.)* I see.

NUN. There so few flowers in the drought. The few in my garden will be gone by the weekend. Fridays I let them take little bouquets home. Everything so brown, these will be . . . *(Realizing no one is listening.)* . . . nice. Nice. *(Nun tries to continue her work quietly, but aware Priest is more annoyed, she takes paper and scissors and puts them on u. table. Nun, unable to find anything to take her attention.)* Would you like to resume the reading lessons after All Saints? *(Nun returns to sit on L. stool.)*

PRIEST. I didn't know you had stopped, Mrs. Shandig.

MRS. SHANDIG. What's the use? There's no time. No time, Father.

NUN. We'll be all cooped up in here when it snows. Some days the children can't even get up the hill they told me. By spring you could be a wonderful reader. *(Silence.)* Why do you burn your lamp so late at night, Mrs. Shandig? It makes a square of light on the ground. *(Nun sits.)*

MRS. SHANDIG. I hear you walking, Sister, so I work on the mending.

NUN. *(Standing.)* I didn't know you could hear me. I pray. Do you ever pray standing up?

MRS. SHANDIG. You must walk when you pray too, Sister.

NUN. I'm sorry. I didn't know you could hear me. *(She waits for someone to speak, then, looking out window.)* I like to look at the few lights down in the valley, try to imagine why those three or four windows have a warm glow so late at night. Someone sick, a party, a student preparing for an exam, a baby being born. Do you ever do that? *(Silence.)* Then I look up at those trees beh'nd the convent. Trees. They catch the stars, darken the ground. It's like you said, Father. I pray against the dark. (*Silence.*) Do you know what I mean, Mrs. Shandig? About praying.

MRS. SHANDIG. I don't know, Sister. You are a nun. I never know what to say about such things. I don't stand when I pray. I didn't think you are supposed to. Are you, Father? I'm sorry. You want to read, don't you?

NUN. It is not disrespectful if you want to pray, Mrs. Shandig. God gave us a brain after all, and I think He expects us to use it.

MRS. SHANDIG. (*Rising, crossing behind Priest.*) Father, I wish Sister wouldn't talk personal like this. I don't understand things the way you do, Sister. (*Silence.*)

NUN. Well, you talk personal with the other sisters. I hear you, Mrs. Shandig.

MRS. SHANDIG. Not blasphemy, Sister.

PRIEST. (*Standing.*) Mrs. Shandig. Let me talk to Sister. We'll say the rosary later.

MRS. SHANDIG. (*As she exits.*) Yes, Father. (*Silence.*)

NUN. Can we, can't we just discuss it?

PRIEST. Don't you know we are very close to serious difficulty?

NUN. No. Why?

PRIEST. We cannot talk like this, Sister.

NUN. We cannot talk. We have not spoken a single word for a month.

PRIEST. Exactly as it should be, Sister.

NUN. No. I'm here, and you've got to let me help you. It's useless to stay locked in your study, striking out at poor Mrs. Shandig when all you need to— I don't live in the convent. I won't be ignored.

PRIEST. I want you to think what you've said. (*Silence.*) Then you tell me. In the Confessional. That is the appropriate place for you to speak to me.

NUN. Well, I suppose it all sounds especially Protestant to your particularly Catholic ears. (*Nun turns to exit. Priest grabs her.*)

PRIEST. Yes, it does. It sounds like, like . . . (*Silence. They face each other for a long moment.*)

NUN. (*Defeated, crossing to window seat.*) I am trying to be a good nun, Father.

PRIEST. I know.

NUN. All of a sudden, this last month, nothing seems the way

I . . . At Guardian Angel, we laughed all the time. And they held you if you cried. Here the sisters talk together in their beds. Then when I get there they have nothing to say to me, and yet they talk to her all the time.

PRIEST. You have the students.

NUN. Yes, Father. I do. I love watching them together, yelling and running down the hill. I almost hope they'll fall and scrape their knees so they'll come to me. That's awful. I didn't know it until I said— I don't know what's wrong with me. If only I could talk things out, it would be so much better. Couldn't we have dinner together again? It's been so long since I ate with any— (*Priest turns chair around so he can sit face-to-face with Nun.*)

PRIEST. We must accept God's Will.

NUN. It couldn't be God's Will that we go out of our way to be unhappy.

PRIEST. One doesn't question God.

NUN. I never question God.

PRIEST. Sometimes I think you want the Church to be imperfect.

NUN. I do not.

PRIEST. You want it to be perfectly human. But humans are imperfect. You cannot bend the Church every which way for temporary reasons.

NUN. Father, I didn't mean—

PRIEST. In Italy the peasants show their penitence by praying as they crawl on their knees up mountainous stone steps to the churches. They have been doing this for hundreds of years. By the time they reach the top the flesh on their legs is ripped, bleeding with small pieces of gravel imbedded in their skins. Bare bone shows through the men's best pants. And they don't complain. They don't snivel. They don't cry. They accept God and His Church. They smile at the top because they know God smiles. He is only satisfied when the pain of your prayer equals His in hearing our pitiful prayers.

NUN. Father, don't—

PRIEST. Don't pray when you're standing. Especially you shouldn't. It's not an appropriate gesture to God for you to make. If you kneel, it will remind you of your humility, your shame and you'll stop questioning every—

NUN. Stop it. Stop. I can't stand this. I can't. (*Silence.*) Have you ever been human? God is perfectly aware I respect and love

41

him, Father. And He knows I am human. Every breath I let out and every movement I make I try to make for Him. And if I felt closer to Him standing on my head when I pray, I would stand on my head.

PRIEST. Christ knelt. (*Nun slaps Priest. He slaps Nun.*)

NUN. How do I— I'm all alone. If there were just one thing about you that was human. I don't believe you have the same blood in your veins as I do. I don't believe it. Do you? Do you bleed when you're cut? There's nothing human about you. (*Priest grabs paring knife, jabs hand, holds it so Nun can see blood, then smears blood on Nun's face.*)

PRIEST. (*Throwing knife on floor.*) Stay away from me. (*Mrs. Shandig, unaware of what has transpired, enters on the striking of the hour, carrying two rosaries. Nun quickly hands her handkerchief to Priest so Mrs. Shandig doesn't notice. Priest wraps bleeding hand. Mrs. Shandig gives Priest his rosary. They kneel, each facing a separate way.*)

PRIEST, NUN and MRS. SHANDIG. (*Crossing themselves.*) In the Name of the Father, the Son and the . . . (*Fast curtain.*)

## ACT II

## THE PARLOR

*Lights come up on Nun, Rivard and Mrs. Shandig pray-*
*ing as they were at the end of Act I. They are saying the*
*Lord's Prayer. When they reach "forgive us our tres-*
*passes. . . ," Rivard stands and calls out. Mrs. Shandig*
*and Nun almost silently complete the prayer.*

## THE CELL

RIVARD. (*Standing.*) Guard. Guard. Can you hear me? Guard.
(*Guard enters from* U. R.)

GUARD. Easy. Easy. You'll wake the whole damn town.

RIVARD. (*Crossing into cell.*) How late is it?

GUARD. After ten-thirty. Is that all you wanted? I'll get you a
clock tomorrow. Damn. (*Nun and Mrs. Shandig exit* U. L.)

RIVARD. (*Sitting on* L. *stool.*) Could you talk with me? For just
a bit.

GUARD. Why?

RIVARD. I can't sleep. Sit down.

GUARD. (*Sitting on* R. *stool.*) So.

RIVARD. I suppose you've heard who the Prosecutor's calling
next.

GUARD. Sure. Why?

RIVARD. You appear to be the kind of young man who knows
what is happening.

GUARD. Erna Prindle. He's calling her.

RIVARD. Why Erna?

GUARD. Why he's desperate of course. He lost everything on
Louise. Old Toby's really giving him a run for his money. Erna
won't be able to say nothing. Maurice Prindle don't like you R.C.'s
He'll beat her black and blue if she lets on how she liked being a
Catholic. Last year you should've seen her carrying trays over here
with her arm broke. Wowie.

43

RIVARD. Amos, I imagine you could figure a way for me to talk with Erna.

GUARD. Sure. Why?

RIVARD. Before she testifies, I could—

GUARD. Oh no. No, Father. Ain't nobody can pull the wool over these eyes.

RIVARD. I want to comfort her, tell her not to stand up for me if Maurice would—

GUARD. Sure. And tell her what you want her to say. Pretend a Confession or something and tell her what to do. I know about you R.C.'s. And, Father, I don't like it. Never did, even before the murder. (*Guard exits* R.)

## ERNA'S PARLOR

(*Nun enters. After a moment, Priest follows her. Silence, tension.*)

NUN. (u. *of small table.*) So this is Erna's. (*Silence. After a moment, Nun discovers a music box and begins playing it. Priest is startled and looks to see what the sound is. Priest crosses* u. l.) Music box. (*Priest turns off music box. Silence. He sits on settee.*)

PRIEST. What you said last night. About me. It is not true.

NUN. (*Sitting on chair.*) I never should— I'm sorry, Father. It was just—

PRIEST. Let me say this before Erna comes back. Then it'll be over; you will forget last night. See, all this, it's your fault. And, I need your help.

NUN. What is my fault?

PRIEST. I can't get done what I should. Here at Erna's I am to comfort her. This is a normal, routine matter for a priest. But I'm so confused that, I know I need help. I have to if I'm to be a good priest. And I want to be. I must say what a good priest—

NUN. I never said you weren't a good priest.

PRIEST. Please, Sister. Hear me out. I can learn, or relearn. I can change. I have already, just saying out loud that I am afraid is a start. I have to tell you that Erna's mother, well, she is going to die. The doctor told me. I have to tell Erna. I have to help her try. And I thought all night about what you think of me, and very early this morning I decided that you should be here, that you would help me make a new start. I thought that if I hear you talk with Erna, I would hear the way you would try to—

44

NUN. You want me to help?

PRIEST. Yes.

NUN. Thank you, Father. (*Erna enters from* L. *She has a handkerchief and is trying not to cry, but is barely succeeding.*)

ERNA. Mama's still sleeping. I checked.

NUN. (*Sitting with Erna on settee.*) My aunt's husband was sick something like your mother, Erna. The same. He stayed like your mother, just sleeping, for five days.

ERNA. But he died. Mama's not going to die.

NUN. But before. That was actually the hardest for me. I was terrified to be in his room, ashamed not to be.

ERNA. I'm afraid she'll hear me crying.

NUN. I know. I tried to keep it inside so my uncle wouldn't hear. Of course, he couldn't. I was much younger than you. I didn't know what was to become of me if he died.

PRIEST. Sister, maybe Erna wouldn't want to hear about this?

ERNA. Oh yes, Father. It's just the same. I have to be quiet too. And I don't know what'll happen either. I just don't. Mama and I, we take care of each other. (*Priest indicates Nun may continue.*)

NUN. When I was in his room, I remember looking out the window. It was spring. I had just planted my garden. And there was a little sparrow at the feeder, but I'd forgotten to put out crumbs for worrying. Suddenly the sparrow flew down to the garden and started eating the seeds I'd planted.

ERNA. That's awful.

NUN. He was hungry. I wondered how he knew to do that. Whatever would make him know there were seeds there? Then I remembered that God watches over all things, even the sparrows. I laughed.

ERNA. (*Crying openly.*) Oh, Sister.

PRIEST. What Sister is saying is that God obviously was watching over her in her trouble. Just as He will watch over you and your mother too, Erna.

NUN. And, of course, that is all I wanted to say, Father.

ERNA. Mama's not going to die, is she?

PRIEST. Your mother's lived a good life. She's a good Catholic. She has nothing to fear. You don't need to cry.

ERNA. (*Standing, embraced by Nun.*) No. No. No. Mama can't die.

45

PRIEST. (*Crossing behind Erna.*) Please, Erna. Listen to me. Crying won't help.

NUN. It can, Father. Just let her—

PRIEST. Erna, you must accept God's will.

ERNA. I don't want to be all alone. She can't die. (*Throwing herself in Nun's arms, crying.*) What would happen to me out here? I'd be all alone.

PRIEST. Erna—

NUN. Father, perhaps, it would be better—

PRIEST. Your mother is in God's hands, isn't she? Don't cry, Erna.

ERNA. (*Turning to Priest.*) But I can't help it. When it starts, I just can't.

PRIEST. Pray for strength, say your rosary. "They who wait upon the Lord shall renew their strength. They shall mount up with wings as eagles, they shall run and not be weary . . . " See, if you try hard enough, you can resist the temptation to—

NUN. To be human? People have to cry, Father. Before you said that you—

PRIEST. Erna. Tears are personal destruction. Destruction of anything is an affront to God.

NUN. But Jesus wept. God was not affronted when His only begot—

PRIEST. Erna, you must accept all of God's world. Not just that which pleases you. Let me tell you a story of when I was a boy. (*Erna sits on R. side of settee.*)

ERNA. Are you from Detroit too, Father? (*Priest sits on settee, Nun on chair.*)

PRIEST. No. I came from a large family, very large. There were so many of us, in fact, that in order to feel important I told strangers I was an only child. But a real problem hit me and my family. Diphtheria. In one winter I saw nine brothers and sisters buried. Also my father. After the first one, the baby, no amount of coaxing could get me to stop crying. Oh yes, I cried, Sister. I could not understand how God allowed such cruelty, those meaningless deaths. Why the baby? Papa? By Christmas I was the oldest brother. The house had been quarantined so I had to help. However, in the sick rooms, I just kept right on crying as if whoever I was serving was already dead. After a visit from me, mother would have to spend an hour in the sick room quieting the patient. Even though we were forbidden to leave the yard, I had to get away. I thought if I ran hard enough and fast enough the tears would dry in my eyes and I would stop crying. I asked God to give me the strength not to cry. He didn't hear me. I sat by the river. I thought it was so useless that it would make no difference if I just relaxed and slid down the steep bank and let myself drown.

ERNA. No, Father.

PRIEST. I thought how can God let things be so bad? After all we know everything is God. He even allows evil so that we can confront it. And then I understood. Even the bad, the ugly, the cruel is part of God. To deny it, any part of it, is to deny God. I understood the world is evil and that unless I confronted it with strength I could never see the face of God. If you persist in believing only in His goodness, then He casts you into everlasting— (*Silence.*) I stopped crying. I returned home and worked hard, harder than even my mother. I went through the crisis nights with a sister and then a brother, and the doctor said I may have saved their lives. As soon as I stopped crying, I became useful to God. I have not cried since then.

ERNA. I don't mean to, Father. When it starts, I just can't . . . I'm sorry.

NUN. Don't apologize.

PRIEST. No. She's right. Erna knows it's better to—

NUN. (*Standing.*) People don't apologize for crying, for feeling. Erna only needs—

PRIEST. (*Standing to leave.*) Sister, this is not the time to discuss—

ERNA. Oh, no, not yet. Don't. Please don't, Father. I'll get the coffee and the muffins. They're the kind you like. (*She exits´ L. Long silence.*)

PRIEST. You should not have spoken as you did in front of Erna.

NUN. You asked me to help you, Father.

PRIEST. You made her cry. Erna is hopeless without the strength and the reason to control—

NUN. She does not need to be a saint.

PRIEST. You leave this place. She does not. She has got to have control.

NUN. She's not crying because she's selfish. She's crying because she's scared. Erna needs to believe she won't be left all alone. That's all she needs.

47

PRIEST. The Church does not exist to meet every sniveling need people have.

NUN. The Church does not despise people and what they do.

PRIEST. While you are in my charge, you will never question me again. (*Priest moves to cell and sits on* R. *stool. Nun crosses and kneels* R. *of chair. In dark at* L., *Guard strikes small table and Lawyer, Prosecutor, Erna and Guard take places in court. Sound of church bell calling people to confession is heard.*)

## THE CONFESSIONAL

NUN. Bless me, Father, for I have sinned. It has been one week since my last confession.

PRIEST. (*Simultaneously.*) In nomine Patris, Fili et Spiritus Sanctus.

NUN. Father, ever since we went out to Erna's farm, I've been trying to understand what I did wrong.

PRIEST. My child, do you think you might have been presumptuous?

NUN. Yes. Every week I confess that imperfection. But there must be more that I should confess.

PRIEST. No. That is all, Sister.

NUN. Then why do you act like I've—

PRIEST. How do I act? This is the Confessional.

NUN. But it is my only chance, Father.

PRIEST. You talk to God here. Only God. Do you hear me?

NUN. Father Rivard gets so angry with me, God. I don't know why. I don't know what he expects of me. I don't know what I do that makes him—

PRIEST. (*Standing.*) No. I'm not hearing it the way I should.

NUN. It's my confession.

PRIEST. (*Crossing to court.*) I don't have the proper attitude of distance.

NUN. (*As Priest exits.*) You can't stop my confession. I have to confess. What will happen? I can't go to Communion. (*Rivard sits with Lawyer on bench or settee. Nun exits* R.)

## THE COURT

PROSECUTOR. Did Father Rivard say a novena after your Mother's death?

48

ERNA. Yes. To St. Jude.

PROSECUTOR. Who is this saint, St. Jude?

ERNA. The patron of hopeless and desperate causes.

PROSECUTOR. Hopeless. Desperate.

ERNA. He said we both needed strength. (*Rivard crosses to cell.*)

PROSECUTOR. The priest needed strength because he was hopeless and desperate.

LAWYER. (*Crossing toward Prosecutor.*) Objection. The Prosecutor is not only leading the witness, he is—

PROSECUTOR. I withdraw the question. Erna, why—

ERNA. For Mama. For Mama. The novena was for Mama. He didn't pray for himself. He prayed for everyone. That's what they do.

PROSECUTOR. Erna. Please. Erna, only answer my questions. If just thinking about novenas is upsetting, we'll talk about something else. Why did you stop being a Catholic?

ERNA. I'm a born Catholic.

PROSECUTOR. In what church were you married?

ERNA. Can't we talk about something else?

PROSECUTOR. (*After court stops laughing, sitting on bench.*) Mrs. Prindle, in which church choir do you sing?

ERNA. I'm a Methodist. But I am Catholic too. I'm raising up the children Catholic as much as can be, Father. I'm teaching them the Rosary. (*Erna puts hands over mouth, shocked at her slip.*)

PROSECUTOR. (*Standing.*) Maurice's children know the Rosary.

ERNA. No. No.

PROSECUTOR. (*Crossing to Erna.*) Does your husband, Maurice, know about rosaries in the house?

RIVARD. Leave her alone. (*Rivard starts to stand, but Lawyer stops him.*)

ERNA. It wasn't wrong to marry him. Maurice is a good man. No other priest ever came to Holy Rosary after Father left.

PROSECUTOR. So that was reason enough to desert—

ERNA. I didn't know what to do.

PROSECUTOR. (*Crossing around Lawyer.*) Erna, how can we understand that a good Catholic girl, who knows all about novenas and saints and heaven knows what, a girl who teaches her Protestant children secretly the rosary . . . how can we understand that she would marry outside the Church?

ERNA. But Sister said there was no reason—

49

PROSECUTOR. Sister Rita.

ERNA. Yes.

PROSECUTOR. (*Crossing to Erna.*) Told you to marry a Methodist.

ERNA. No. No, you don't know how it was.

PROSECUTOR. (*Right up to Erna.*) How was it then, Erna?

ERNA. After Mama died, I was teaching Sister some handwork. On the day of the fire, I came in and brought her some jonquil bulbs and to work with her, and she told me it was all right to go to the Methodist socials. That's all.

PROSECUTOR. To look for a husband?

ERNA. There weren't any unmarried men who were Catholics?

PROSECUTOR. And you hooked Maurice, right?

ERNA. No. No, it wasn't like that.

PROSECUTOR. Erna, as a former Catholic, would you expect a good nun to encourage a mixed marriage?

RIVARD. Make him stop. (*Lawyer quiets Rivard.*)

ERNA. I'm still Catholic, and Sister was a good—

PROSECUTOR. Not Sister Rita. Any nun. Does a good nun break the Church rules? Yes or no?

ERNA. No.

PROSECUTOR. Yet Sister Rita wanted you to marry a Methodist.

ERNA. I was all alone. She only told me I could go there to the socials. I didn't know what to do. I was all alone out on the farm. There were sounds at night. Sounds I never heard before. And I was going to be an old maid. I'm not very pretty you know. I'm not. You don't know. I had to do what I could. Father? Father? (*Erna stands, holds arms out to Rivard, held back by Guard.*)

RIVARD. (*Standing, starting toward Erna, held by Lawyer.*) Leave her alone. Leave her alone. This cruelty must stop. (*Erna sits.*)

PROSECUTOR. (*Crossing around bench.*) If the defendant wishes to make a statement he must be under oath.

LAWYER. Objection.

RIVARD. Now. Not after the verdict. Now.

PROSECUTOR. I want this in the record.

RIVARD. Listen to me. I was there, but I didn't help. (*Silence, as he crosses to comfort Erna.*)

LAWYER. I move this Court be adjourned until such time— (*Following simultaneously.*)

RIVARD. Enough cruelty has happened.

LAWYER. This is inadmissable.

RIVARD. This cruelty must not happen because of me.

PROSECUTOR. I want this in the record.

RIVARD. No, don't. I'm innocent of all that.

LAWYER. Rivard.

RIVARD. I know I was wrong.

LAWYER. He's not under oath. This doesn't count.

RIVARD. But he is destroying these people who've come to help me.

PROSECUTOR. Everything I'm doing is to get to the bottom of the crime. (*Lawyer takes Rivard to sit on bench.*)

RIVARD. (*Lunging at Prosecutor.*) Everything I did was for the Church. He is trying to destroy Erna. (*Rivard punches Prosecutor in stomach. Guard grabs Rivard.*)

LAWYER. Take him out. Amos, take him. (*Guard takes Rivard to cell.*)

PROSECUTOR. (*Exiting* L.) I will call no more witnesses. The Prosecution rests. (*Lawyer sits on chair* L. *as Guard throws Rivard into cell with Nun.*)

## NUN'S GARDEN

(*Nun, wearing a shawl to ward off autumn cold, sits on ground, and singing the "Lilac Song." He walks to Nun, enjoys watching her.*)

SISTER RITA. (*Singing.*) *

Spring brings promises in the lilacs,
Dreams of lavendar and green.
When I hide myself in lilacs,
Winter's madness seems a dream.
The scent of the lilacs like a gentle wind;
The touch of the flowers like a baby's hand.
Oh lilac, you can grow when the earth is cold.
You are here when no one knows.

PRIEST. You sound happy. (*Sister Rita continues singing.*) I've come here to your garden many times. Just to th:nk. I will miss it this winter.

NUN. So will I.

* See note at back of playbook.

51

PRIEST. (*Crossing down ramp.*) Did you watch the sunrise? (*Silence.*)

NUN. (*Standing.*) I don't want to detain you.

PRIEST. (*Sitting on edge of* C.) I have time. This is a bit of a celebration today. In a sense. You see I am finished with the book. Forever.

NUN. (*Sitting on* L. *stool.*) You did; it's . . . I'm so used to you being busy, Father.

PRIEST. What are you thinking?

NUN. (*Tatting.*) The lilacs will survive the drought. Maurice told me. He's going to give me some lilacs from behind his shop next spring.

PRIEST. How is it that you talked to Maurice?

NUN. He let me go with him to Traverse City.

PRIEST. When? I didn't give you permission.

NUN. I have to go there for Confession. (*Silence.*)

PRIEST. What are you doing?

NUN. Tatting. Erna taught me.

PRIEST. You don't think you spend too much time outside the Church, do you?

NUN. Father, I took responsibility for my well being a month ago at confession. Helping Erna does not interfere with my teaching or other responsibilities. Erna and I are friends. I think I understand her. She feels quite unloved, useless without her mother.

PRIEST. Sister, I am only concerned that you might waste time—

NUN. (*Standing, preparing to leave.*) I intend to waste even more time on Erna. I don't really care what you do or think.

PRIEST. Please. Don't talk like that.

NUN. I know what it's like for Erna day after day. Night after night. Those dreadful stripes on my bedroom wall. It's like a prison. I can't sleep. I can't breathe. I have to get out and walk in the hall up there.

PRIEST. (*Standing, walking up ramp.*) The same wallpaper is all through the house. In my room too. (*Silence.*) Let Erna to go the Methodist socials.

NUN. What do you mean, Father?

PRIEST. Let her go. Maybe you shouldn't say that I am allowing it. Otherwise, everyone in the parish—

NUN. Thank you, Father. I'll tell her. Thank you. (*Putting her hand on his arm.*) I can't even say how I feel. That you're helping

Erna. That you finished your book. That maybe now you'll have time for— That we could— That you'll bring me that lilac bush from the valley you promised. (*They laugh.*) I, I'd like to read your book.

PRIEST. I destroyed it.

NUN. What?

PRIEST. I'll never leave here. I burned it.

NUN. Why, Father?

PRIEST. Well. I thought I knew God. God, the Vengeful. The God of Job. That God, He was the one I set out to write about. Then you came, and tried to fit into what I know the things you said, the things you— It wasn't possible. I don't know God now.

NUN. To destroy it. Your life's work.

PRIEST. Sister, I am fit for nothing more than this small parish. If this. And I will have to fight to be worthy of this.

NUN. I couldn't have said anything so bad that you'd destroy it because of me.

PRIEST. (*As both sit on stools.*) Because of, or for you. What difference does it make? Maybe God is only hope. Why else do you and I keep promising each other such senseless hopes? No one ever gets what he works for, what he wants. That's God's order. See, I didn't know that before you came. You taught me.

NUN. Oh no, no, no. Every night. I've had this conversation a hundred times. Every night I couldn't sleep. I expected it all differently.

PRIEST. (*Standing.*) What else did you expect?

NUN. (*Standing.*) I don't know. I don't know. (*Nun exits. Rivard sits on* L. *stool.*)

## THE CELL

LAWYER. (*Crossing to cell.*) Listen, you son of a bitch, what are you doing to me?

RIVARD. What? What do you mean?

LAWYER. Standing up, talking like some crazy man in the court.

RIVARD. That was for Erna.

LAWYER. Rivard. Look, you know I never argued an actual trial before. Not like this. Hell, I never even cross-examined a witness before.

RIVARD. You've done it well.

53

LAWYER. I know. But, Rivard, I need your help. I can't do it alone and on top of everything I've found out you lied to me.

RIVARD. I never lied to you.

LAWYER. (*Taking letter from pocket.*) There was a light up at Holy Rosary very late last night, just like there used to be. I went up. I found this. (*Rivard paces in cell.*) "Bishop, I beg that you transfer Sister Rita. I know now I shall never leave this place. Sister does live in the rectory. I made her lie to the Monsignor for my own selfish reasons. Sister has a way about her, and it makes me think I am loving her. I know I must run from this temptation, and I do, but I grow weary. Very weary." (*Lawyer sits.*) You wrote it, but you didn't mail it.

RIVARD. But I wrote it the last day. It was too late.

LAWYER. Too late for what?

RIVARD. Please stop. I don't want to remember anymore.

LAWYER. Then change your plea. It'll be easier for you, and I do not know what else to do. See then I could probably get it down to second degree.

RIVARD. Murder.

LAWYER. Reduce the charge. Second degree murder. Second degree would be the most they could give you, and as a matter of fact—

RIVARD. No. She's dead. There are no degrees in death.

LAWYER. But they won't hang you. That's what matters, isn't it?

RIVARD. No, it's not. Please. I don't care if I live or die. I just want to remain sane.

LAWYER. (*Taking a small whiskey flask from his pocket.*) You're sane. You proved that standing up in court. Asking for some room there to be left over for common human decency. And when you did that you put a rope right round your neck. (*He takes a swallow. Rivard refuses the offered whiskey.*) At least you're saner than the crazies up here. They drink and spit, plant and wait, sit and stare. After a while the pupils in their eyes seem to enlarge so that all they can see clearly are gravestones, and two-headed calves, and the wounds of the horses which they themselves back into unseen equipment. They are past care, so I argue their deeds and wills, travel to Leland to see lantern slides of European castles and wonder how men lost the ability to dream and accomplish. And I fish. Mainly I fish. But you, Rivard, you make me wonder about what a man might do. I didn't care much about you, one way or

54

the other when I first saw you. But I care 'cause I s'pose I know that you're a tad like me. And I figure you're worth saving. 'Course maybe now I'm just madder than them. I want to help you. I think I can. Let me change your plea so you can live.

RIVARD. I can't do that.

LAWYER. I hope you bear up then. 'Cause somehow I'm going to find out 'bout that last night. The night of the fire.

RIVARD. All right, counselor. We have to. (*Rivard reaches for whiskey. Smiles. Takes a hefty swallow.*)

LAWYER. They still haven't found Shandig. Some hunters said they saw a woman living out in an old deserted loggers' camp last fall. Maybe that's her. I know she's still in the area 'cause she comes into Solon a couple of times every year. She trades muskrat skins. Now I'm thinking she might be back up at Holy Rosary. Somebody's there. Lights on. House all cleaned up, and your cassock was laying out on the bed. Yes. Mrs. Shandig expects you back, Rivard. That's for sure. (*Starting to exit.*) Yeah, I'm going up there.

RIVARD. (*To Lawyer.*) I tried to save Sister. I did try to save her. (*Toby exits R. Fire alarm bells ring. Stage is flooded in the light of a fire. Nun appears U. in silhouette. Priest takes off jacket. Nun runs to cell. She is wearing a street dress.*)

NUN. (*Calling as she runs, looking everywhere for Priest.*) Father. Father.

## RECTORY FRONT PORCH

NUN. (*Afraid to touch him, but needing to.*) Mrs. Shandig told me you were hurt in town fighting the fire.

PRIEST. It's only my leg. It's a bit hard to stand. I couldn't run well enough if the fire turned so I came back up.

NUN. Maurice said the town is saved, but the farmlands will burn to the bay. The fire almost reached Holy Rosary but they stopped it by digging a fire ditch.

PRIEST. What are you wearing?

NUN. I had to put it on. Down in the town. There were all those flying cinders. My robe caught fire.

PRIEST. Are you hurt?

NUN. No. It's Sophie's mother's.

55

PRIEST. (*Sitting on* L. *stool.*) Aren't you tired? I'm so tired. I think that must be why I fell and twisted—

NUN. (*Kneeling beside him, wiping dirt from his forehead.*) I was so afraid— There's dirt all over you.

PRIEST. (*Taking her hand from his face.*) Please. You shouldn't be out of your habit. When we're so tired, you shouldn't be out of your habit. Go inside and change.

NUN. It's only us. Everyone else is down there. I have this feeling. And it's us. I know it's only us. What is it? It's not knowing that hurts so much. If I could understand, if I could, then it would be all right again. I could do what is right. But I don't know. Please help. (*Nun sits on* R. *stool.*)

PRIEST. The Bishop will help. I wrote him today. I asked that you be transferred.

NUN. No, not that. I'll never know.

PRIEST. We don't want to.

NUN. I want to. All my life I'll wonder.

PRIEST. No. You'll forget. Go upstairs. Now.

NUN. How could I . . . how could I be so wrong?

PRIEST. (*Standing.*) Don't do this.

NUN. I felt this, [and . . . I wish I'd die.]

PRIEST. Go up. Pray.

NUN. (*Crossing to him.*) I can't.

PRIEST. Save us. (*Nun runs inside, up to bench, takes diary, moves* L. *stool up to lean on as she kneels looking out window. Priest kneels to pray* D. L. *in cell.*) Holy Mother, hear me. Gentle Jesus. God. Am I in Your image? God, make me strong. I doubt. I doubt everything. "They who wait upon the Lord shall renew their strength." I am waiting, God. I have always waited. Help me. God, help me. God?

## NUN'S ROOM

NUN. (*At window.*) Where is my garden? The fire ditch. They dug the fire ditch right through my garden. All the bulbs are dug up. The roses. They burned. (*During Nun's speech, Priest abruptly enters, crosses to Nun. Priest holds Nun until sobbing subsides. Nun falls to knees in front of Priest who sits on stool.*)

PRIEST. At night I wonder how you are feeling, what you think, if you're happy, if you can sleep. Even when I pray, I wonder what you're doing. I look up through a window if it's recess or listen for your steps in the hall. I can only concentrate if I pray about you. Almost to you. (*He is about to kiss her.*)

NUN. Please. Tell me what it is.

PRIEST. I have. (*Silence.*) I love you. (*They kiss, stand and embrace.*)

NUN. (*Sitting on stool as Priest sits on bench.*) I never dared think— I thought who else would have me but the Church? But with you I'm nothing, am I?

PRIEST. No. You're not.

NUN. (*Standing to put diary away.*) I'm just like everyone else.

PRIEST. What's that?

NUN. (*Starting to pass Priest.*) Just my diary. I always keep it in the drawer. But it's all right now, isn't it? (*Handing it to Priest.*) Do you want to read it?

PRIEST. It's drawings.

NUN. Not all of it. (*She sits on bench with Priest to look at diary.*)

PRIEST. No. Of course not. This can't be Sister Immaculata, can it?

NUN. I think she must have been in a grump that day.

PRIEST. Every day. Did you show her this?

NUN. No one's ever seen it. I offered to show it to Mother Vincent, but she said the only sin it could possibly be is boring.

PRIEST. She was wrong. This is so easy. Why was I so stupid? I don't understand why it seemed so worthy to—

NUN. Why do we have to understand? Has trying to understand been so wonderful?

PRIEST. No.

NUN. Who's that?

PRIEST. Me? Well, you sure got the eyelashes. [How could you know how I'd look without a beard.

NUN. I guessed.

PRIEST. Well, you'd be disappointed.

NUN. I don't think so.]

PRIEST. You make me so happy. And you made me so miserable.

NUN. I never meant to. (*Leading Priest to window, still holding diary.*) Look. Where I stood all those nights. See. We can be with all the other people now. We aren't so different after all, are

57

we? Don't look at the Church. Look down there with the other families. We'll be like that too.

PRIEST. We can't move down there.

NUN. We'll have our own children.

PRIEST. Children.

NUN. Oh yes. I should have known. Oh, all those nights. Known that if the Church wasn't everything, that you would give me something in its place. [I think I always knew I was not a true Bride of Christ.]

PRIEST. You thought of this before.

NUN. No. Just the confusion. In there you'll see. I just didn't know.

PRIEST. What did you write?

NUN. It doesn't matter, does it?

PRIEST. Read it to me.

NUN. Someday, whenever, you can read it all—

PRIEST. Read it to me. Now. Read it.

NUN. (Looking as she sits on stool.) Well, any page these last few weeks. "I think Father Rivard must be right. Maybe the Church is only for rules, but God is for people. According to the rules everything I feel is wrong, yet nothing feels wrong. Do I have a conscience? Yes, I do. Do I belong in the Church? I don't know. He makes me so confused."

PRIEST. We can never lose our faith.

NUN. We won't.

PRIEST. You can't even think of it.

NUN. (Standing.) Now look. The lights are going on in their homes. We can think of that. We'll be down there and then— (Priest suddenly pulls her from window R.) What is it?

PRIEST. Mrs. Shandig is coming up the hill.

NUN. But we can tell her. Everyone.

PRIEST. No.

NUN. Why?

PRIEST. (Moving to exit.) Because I, I—I'm their priest. She depends on me. They all do. I'm the only way they have of understanding.

NUN. People understand. (She crosses to stop his exit. He grabs her by the arms.)

PRIEST. It's not how you think it is. Their homes have photographs of babies in coffins. Adolescents pour kerosene on kittens, and their fathers laugh when they set the fire. Sometimes wives cannot cook breakfast. Their fingers are broken from their husbands' beatings. It's only because they think I'm different; it's only because they think I'm worthy that I can help them. I must be worthy.

NUN. (*Putting arms around his neck.*) I think you're worthy. Please. You said you loved me. I know you're too good, too precious to escape, desert me when—

PRIEST. I'm not, not what you think. I, I, I've destroyed all that. For the Church. (*Pushing her onto stool.*) There's nothing left for you. I can't be a husband. I can't be (*Kneeling in front of her.*) be a father. There's nothing left but cruelty. That's all I know. That's all I worship. All I need. Not the resurrection, life. It's the nails. My salvation. Only the agony. There's no chance for—

NUN. You're not cruel. It'll be different now.

PRIEST. Damn you. Trying to break me down, make me forget. (*Taking her head in his hands, forcing her to look out window.*) Planting those flowers out there as if you, you could make the world beautiful. What makes you think you could change anything? Promising me things will be better. You make them worse. It's not my fault you lost your faith. It's not. You never had any if it dies so easily. (*He starts to rip up diary. She wrestles it from him.*)

NUN. No. That was before. You can stop. That's gone. It's gone.

PRIEST. (*Grabbing Nun by shoulders, shaking her with violence, causing her to drop diary.*) With them, with them, I can make it look all right. They only want me to say those words. They don't want to know me. You can't know me. I'll destroy you. You can't know me. You'd hate me. I hate myself.

NUN. I don't hate you. God doesn't hate you.

PRIEST. (*Trying to exit.*) Don't talk about God.

NUN. (*Holding him from exit.*) We still have God.

PRIEST. I don't want God. I don't want you. (*Starting to choke Nun.*) I hate God. I hate God. I want to kill God. I always wanted to kill— (*Nun falls on floor. For a moment of silence, she appears dead. Priest slaps her on back. She coughs. He drags her to bench. He gets wet cloth, sits next to her, wiping her brow. Mrs. Shandig begins to enter up ramp. She is looking back down in the valley to see if fire is out.*)

NUN. (*As she stops choking.*) I'm sorry. I'm sorry. What you said. Hating God. It's my fault too. You couldn't—

59

PRIEST. No. No. It's me. (*Mrs. Shandig enters.*)

NUN. We have to help each other. It's all we have now. We only have each other. (*Priest crosses* R. *as he sees Mrs. Shandig.*)

MRS. SHANDIG. (*Moving to hold Nun.*) Sister. What are you saying?

NUN. Please. Mrs. Shandig. Leave us alone.

MRS. SHANDIG. What is wrong? What you said . . . (*Nun throws herself into Mrs. Shandig's arms for comfort.*)

NUN. Tell her. Please tell her.

MRS. SHANDIG. Tell me what?

NUN. Tell her.

MRS. SHANDIG. Tell me what?

NUN. (*Turning from embrace to Priest.*) Just tell her, and it will be over. Please. Tell her you love me. (*Silence as Mrs. Shandig goes, sits on stool.*)

MRS. SHANDIG. Sister. No. No.

PRIEST. There'll be a train. I'll walk to Traverse City. The fire didn't affect the trains there.

NUN. I'll go with you.

PRIEST. No.

MRS. SHANDIG. Father, you can't go.

NUN. (*Suddenly embracing Priest.*) Don't leave me. I don't care if I go to hell.

MRS. SHANDIG. (*Pulling Nun from Priest.*) Father, you hear her. (*About to hit Nun.*) Don't touch him.

PRIEST. (*Catching Mrs. Shandig's hand.*) Stop it. (*Nun crosses to Priest. Both sit on bench.*) I won't hurt you anymore. You can leave. But you must leave the right way, when your community tells you. Go back to your order.

NUN. I'm not a nun now. I'm nothing.

PRIEST. There's still a place for you. They need you.

NUN. I haven't even said it to you.

PRIEST. Don't say anything. Don't think it. Honor your vows. It's the only way. (*Mrs. Shandig backs, unnoticed by audience, to witness chair, where she sits at end of scene.*) The rest is me. I cause it. God isn't cruel.

NUN. (*Crying, hitting Priest.*) No. No. No. There's nothing left. (*As Priest crosses to cell and sits on* R. *stool.*) But I never told you. You never heard the words. Let me tell you. (*Nun crosses* U. *of* L. *stool to watch Priest "walk down hill."*)

MRS. SHANDIG. Father walked down the hill. Sister watched from her window til he was almost out of sight, and then she screamed after him.

NUN. I love you.

MRS. SHANDIG. He didn't even hear her. (*Nun exits* R. *Lawyer walks into Mrs. Shandig's light* L. *of* C. *Prosecutor and Guard enter* U. L. *and watch.*)

LAWYER. Now I want to understand this clearly, Mrs. Shandig.

MRS. SHANDIG. Yes, sir.

LAWYER. When she called to him, he did not turn back.

MRS. SHANDIG. No, sir. He's a priest.

LAWYER. He did not return that night.

MRS. SHANDIG. No, sir. Never.

LAWYER. Did anyone else, anyone come up the hill that night?

MRS. SHANDIG. Maurice came up.

LAWYER. What did he do?

MRS. SHANDIG. He planted a small lilac bush from the town. He told me Father paid him to do it.

LAWYER. Did Maurice see Sister Rita?

MRS. SHANDIG. I don't know.

LAWYER. Now, think. Did Sister see Maurice?

MRS. SHANDIG. Sister went to her garden. She saw the lilac. She touched it, just like she was always touching things and then she went all crazy. She threw herself down on the ground, crying and sort of rolling back and rolling back and forth. She rolled herself right into the ditch they'd dug to stop the fire and she didn't get up. She just lay there in the ditch shaking, like deep sobbing, staring up at me with dead eyes.

LAWYER. I see. I see what you mean. Then what did you do?

MRS. SHANDIG. I prayed to St. Jude for strength and guidance. He answered my prayer, because I understood the lilac was a sign from Father. He paid Maurice to plant the lilac as a sign to me to bury her in the garden. She was too evil to put in the cemetery. I looked at her down there like a snake. She was laying there just like a dead snake. I know that look. When I was a girl, my mother, she saw a snake in the yard. She took a hatchet and ran into the yard and chopped it all up.* It kept wiggling after it was dead. All the pieces moved. I didn't know then that they kept moving until the sun set. She was wiggling down there and making noises, but it was near on to the moonrise, so I knew she was dead. I went to get the shovel. I scraped the dirt back into the fire ditch over her dead wiggling body. I was nearly finished when the dirt over her started to rise. The earth didn't want her body, but I hit the snake's head and shoveled the dirt faster on its face and then it was peaceful. The moon came up and Holy Rosary was silvery and white again, and the fire was far, far away.

LAWYER. (*Addressing audience as court.*) I move this case be dismissed on the grounds that the People's case can not support a verdict of guilty beyond a reasonable doubt. (*Mrs. Shandig looks at Rivard. Guard crosses to her with his handcuffs clearly in sight. He touches her arm. She looks at him confused. He leads her to exit L. Prosecutor exits L.*)

## GRAVESIDE

(*There is the distant, haunting sound of a train whistle. Lawyer crosses to cell, picking up stool used in bedroom scene and putting it back in cell.*)

LAWYER. Rivard. Whew. This hill's too much for me. (*He sits on L. stool. Both he and Rivard on R. stool look straight out.*) So this is where Sister Rita was buried.

RIVARD. Yes.

LAWYER. Rivard. Mrs. Shandig killed herself at the jail. Banged her head against the wall till she died.

RIVARD. No, no. It will not stop.

LAWYER. (*Reaching out to touch Rivard's shoulder.*) I'm sorry. Sorry I called Shandig, and sorry I thought I was so damned clever. At least, you can have forgiveness in your Church, can't you?

RIVARD. Not unless you know God. She gave me a chance. Will I never see the Face of God?

LAWYER. What are you planning you'll do, Rivard?

RIVARD. What are you going to do?

* Alternative speech: "I know that look. When I was a girl, I had a snake. My mother saw me playing with it. She took a hatchet and ran into the yard and chopped it all up."

LAWYER. Fish. Mainly I fish.

RIVARD. Mourn her. Mainly I'll mourn her. (*Rivard reaches for a branch of lilac in bloom on the ground. Lawyer stands and steps slightly back, his head bowed. Nun enters in street dress, coming up ramp.\* Rivard kneels. At the moment he could see her face. He looks up into her face. She stops for a moment and continues up ramp to* U. C. *As the Nun continues. Priest begins to cry. Lawyer takes a step toward him. BLACKOUT.*)

*\* Nun did not appear at end in Broadway production, but this device may be useful in some productions.*

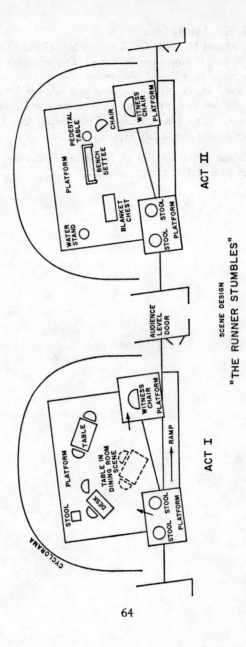

SCENE DESIGN

"THE RUNNER STUMBLES"

ACT I

ACT II

CYCLORAMA

STOOL

PLATFORM

DESK

TABLE IN
DINING ROOM
SCENE

TABLE

WITNESS
CHAIR
PLATFORM

RAMP

STOOL STOOL
PLATFORM

AUDIENCE
LEVEL
DOOR

WATER
STAND

BLANKET
CHEST

PLATFORM

BENCH
SETTEE

PEDESTAL
TABLE

CHAIR

WITNESS
CHAIR
PLATFORM

STOOL
PLATFORM

STOOL

## NOTE ON MUSIC

The lyrics for "The Lilac Song," which are included in the text of *The Runner Stumbles*, were written by the author, Milan Stitt, and may me used in amateur productions of the play without payment of an additional fee. However, as the Play Service is not authorized to suggest specific music for use with these lyrics, it is suggested that producing groups devise appropriate music of their own to be used in their presentations of the play.

## ERRATUM

. Groups producing this play should make the following changes in the text of the Dramatists Play Service edition:

1.) *Page 57*: In the second speech of the NUN, the last sentence should read: "But with you I'm not nothing, am I?" The word "not" was omitted from the published text.

2.) *Page 17*: The first speech of the LAWYER should read: "Objection. The Prosecution is attempting to seek—what do you call it?" The phrase which follows, *privileged communication between the clergyman and the penitent* was inadvertently included in the published text and should be deleted.

3.) *Page 30*: In the speech of the PRIEST at the top of the page (which began on page 29) the sentence beginning on the sixth line should read: "The Church makes my life, any life possible." The word "any" was misprinted as "and" in the published text.

4.) *Pages 22 and 23*: The three line scene in THE STUDY should be eliminated.

# FURNITURE LIST

## ACT I

THE CELL:
2 stools

COURTROOM:
Witness chair-swivel

STUDY:
Desk
2 chairs
1 footstool

KITCHEN:
1 long table
1 chair

## ACT II

*Erna's:*
Settee (doubles as court bench)
Pedestal table
Chair

*Nun's Room:*
Trunk
Washstand

# PROPERTY PLOT

## ACT I

Handcuffs
Set of keys (Guard)
Napkin with muffins (Erna)
Envelope and pencil (Toby)
Suitcase (Nun)
Bunch of lilacs (Nun)
Bowl of bread dough (Shandig)
Towel (Shandig)
Tray (Shandig)
Bread kneading board (Shandig)

Mug
Nutmeg
Sugar bowl (on tea tray)
Egg
Wooden spoon
Book (Nun)
Children's compositions (Nun)
Small notebook (Prosecutor)
Manuscript
Pens
Cigar box and cigars
Matches
Inkwell
Ashtray
Folder of children's paintings
large tray
2 forks, knives, spoons, napkins
Tablecloth
Bread board
Bread
Wine decanter
2 glasses
2 bowls stew
A few wild flowers
2 mugs of egg nog
large basket
Garden hat
Large tray (tea tray)
Teapot
Sugar bowl (in kitchen)
Cream pitcher
3 cups and saucers
Teaspoon
Bowl of beans
Apron
Harness
Rag
Brown paper
Scissors
Bowl of apples
1 paring knife
1 trick paring knife
2 rosaries
Letter from the Bishop in envelope
Missal

Music box
Confession stole
Basket
Tatting bobbin
Garden gloves
Letter to Bishop
Linen towel
Pitcher and bowl
Whiskey flask
Diary
Lilac branch

# COSTUME PLOT

**Rivard:**
Cuff links
Black check jacket
Black check vest
2 grey and tan striped shirts with white collar band
Dark grey trousers
Suspenders
Socks (2 pair)
Black boots
Rosary

**Sister Rita:**
Nun's habit: robe, belt, 2 piece wimple, veil
Rosary
Black shoes
Pantyhose (2 pair)
Wedding ring
Black shawl
Lavender-grey print dress with belt
Petticoat

**Mrs. Shandig:**
Long black slip
Grey wool dress
Pantyhose (2 pair)
Leather belt
Check apron
Rust sweater
Straw hat
Brown boots
Rosary

**Toby Felker:**
Suspenders
2 blue stripe shirts
2 white collars
Black string tie
Cuff links
Check vest
Brown tweed suit

69

Watch chain
Socks (2 pair)
Brown shoes
Green cap
Red plaid Mackinaw

*Prosecutor:*
3 piece grey tweed suit
Suspenders
Green tie
Tie tack
Cuff links
2 dotted shirts with white collar
Socks (2 pair)
Pocket watch and chain
Black shoes

*Erna Prindle:*
Green plaid dress with belt
Brooch—cameo
Brown striped apron
Petticoat
Beige shawl
Black print headscarf
Pantyhose (2 pair)
Black shoes
Handkerchief

*Monsignor Nicholson:*
Wire-frame glasses
Black clerical dickey
White clerical collars (2)
Cuff links
Suspenders
2 piece black suit
2 white shirts
Socks (2 pair)
Black shoes

*Louise:*
Tan blouse
Blue jumper
Blue cape
Brown muff
Pantyhouse (2 pair)

70

Brown pumps
Petticoat
Hair bow

*Guard:*
Wool plaid shirt
Long underwear top
Grey tweed trousers
Suspenders
Socks (2 pair)
Brown work shoes

*New*

PLAYS

CHILDREN OF A LESSER GOD

PASSIONE

G. R. POINT

TIME AND GINGER

FATHERS AND SONS

THREE SISTERS

FULL MOON

THE ORPHANS

DUCK HUNTING

THE UBU PLAYS

TENNESSEE

THE COAL DIAMOND

WOMEN STILL WEEP

THE EXHIBITION

 **DRAMATISTS PLAY SERVICE, INC.**

440 Park Avenue South    New York, N. Y. 10016

# New
# PLAYS

**HOME**

**CLOTHES FOR A SUMMER HOTEL**

**KID CHAMPION**

**MARIE AND BRUCE**

**HIDE AND SEEK**

**JOSEPHINE: THE MOUSE SINGER**

**THE GIRLS OF THE GARDEN CLUB**

**UNCLE VANYA**

**THE PALACE AT 4 A.M.**

**SISTER MARY IGNATIUS EXPLAINS IT ALL FOR YOU**

**BAG LADY**

**COMPANIONS OF THE FIRE**

**CINDERELLA WORE COMBAT BOOTS**

**DRAMATISTS PLAY SERVICE, INC.**
440 PARK AVENUE SOUTH          NEW YORK, N.Y. 10016

# New
# PLAYS

**THE AMERICAN CLOCK**

**CHILDE BYRON**

**CLOSE OF PLAY**

**THE TRADING POST**

**THE LEGENDARY STARDUST BOYS**

**CLOSE TIES**

**OPAL'S MILLION DOLLAR DUCK**

**IN FIREWORKS LIE SECRET CODES**

**STOPS ALONG THE WAY**

**VILLAINOUS COMPANY**

**THE ACTOR'S NIGHTMARE**

Inquiries Invited

**DRAMATISTS PLAY SERVICE, INC.**

440 Park Avenue South          New York, N. Y. 10016

# RECENT

 *Releases* . . .

ALBUM

MIXED COUPLES

THE CAPTIVITY
   OF PIXIE SHEDMAN

BACK IN THE RACE

THE TANTALUS

STILL LIFE

BEAUTY AND THE BEAST
   (Children's play)

THYMUS VULGARIS

LIMBO TALES (3 short plays)

THE FORMER ONE-ON-ONE
   BASKETBALL CHAMPION

THE TERRIBLE TATTOO PARLOR

*Write for information as to
availability*

## DRAMATISTS PLAY SERVICE, Inc.

440 Park Avenue South          New York, N. Y. 10016

Ne

TITLES

CRIMES OF THE HEART
KEY EXCHANGE
THE HOTHOUSE

440